MW00777693

Turn the Page

TURNING FROM DARKNESS TO LIGHT
THROUGH CHRIST JESUS

Anne Maxwell

TRILOGY CHRISTIAN PUBLISHERS

TUSTIN, CA

Trilogy Christian Publishers
A Wholly Owned Subsidiary of Trinity Broadcasting Network
2442 Michelle Drive
Tustin, CA 92780

For information, address Trilogy Christian Publishing

Rights Department, 2442 Michelle Drive, Tustin, Ca 92780.

Trilogy Christian Publishing/ TBN and colophon are trademarks of Trinity Broadcasting Network.

For information about special discounts for bulk purchases, please contact Trilogy Christian Publishing.

Manufactured in the United States of America

Trilogy Disclaimer: The views and content expressed in this book are those of the author and may not necessarily reflect the views and doctrine of Trilogy Christian Publishing or the Trinity Broadcasting Network.

10 9 8 7 6 5 4 3 2 1

Library of Congress Cataloging-in-Publication Data is available.
ISBN 978-1-64773-741-2
ISBN 978-1-64773-742-9 (ebook)

Dedication

This book is dedicated to my son, Max.

Acknowledgement

If not for the Holy Spirit, I would still be heading down the wrong path. Our Heavenly Father is always patient, loving, and encouraging, and I finally understand what unconditional love and forgiveness truly mean.

I can't fully express my appreciation, gratitude and love for my son. Max is the reason for my journey and quest to become a better person and follower of Jesus Christ. He endured all of my ups and downs, successes and failures, including depression, addiction, divorce and health issues.

Also, I want to acknowledge my dearest friend Joi, who has shown me unconditional love for over fifty years. A sister in Christ, she taught me what a true friend looks like. I look forward to working with her company, Marcum Media, to promote this book.

There are so many biblical teachers that have helped me through my journey. The most influential being Charles Stanley of In Touch Ministries, who has taught me how to live a godly life. For thirty-five years, I have listened to him teach the word of God and taken notes, which I referred to often while writing this book. In no particular order are many other evangelists that have helped me along my journey: Creflo Dollar, David Jerimiah, Billy Graham, Pat Robertson, June Hunt, D. James Kennedy, J. Vernon McGee, James Dobson, Jack Graham, Betty and James Robinson, Andrew Wommack, Jack Laurie, John Hagee, T.D. Jakes, Gregory Dickow, Tony Evans, Dr. Ed Young, Michael Youssef, Robert Morris, and Chuck Swindoll. Each one of them has encouraged me at different times in my life, and I listen to them as often as possible.

My deepest appreciation to Terry Meeuwsen from CBN 700 Club, who received a word of knowledge on November 1, 2019. I was diagnosed with Ulcerative Colitis Disease in December of 2016 and suffered greatly from the effects of that disease. On that morning, during the 700 Club broadcast, Terry spoke directly to me and claimed healing over my disease! This miracle made it possible for me to finish my manuscript.

Finally, please let me express my gratitude to the reader of this book. I pray that it helps you along your spiritual path and moves you out of darkness and into the light.

Foreword

I have struggled with manic depression my entire life. Even in my childhood, I remember feeling the "highest of highs" and the "lowest of lows," and that mirrors how my life has gone. Living with the effects of manic depression, I started "self-medicating" with drugs and alcohol at a very young age. This led me down a very dark path of addiction and deeper depression.

I didn't truly surrender my life to Christ until I was almost forty. In an attempt to save my marriage, I attended a workshop at the Catholic Diocese in Dallas, Texas. During this weekend encounter, the Holy Spirit entered my heart, and God started changing my path. This began a twenty-year journey of reading the Bible, studying and meditating on God's word.

Because of my reluctance to let go of control and trying to do things "my own way," the journey has not been easy. Even filled with the Holy Spirit, I continued to struggle with ups and downs, darkness and light, failures and accomplishments. Finally, I understand that life is a journey, but God offers us a much easier path when we surrender to Him and seek His will. Through Him, we can defeat depression, addiction and every other strife in our lives.

This book highlights stories of people throughout the Bible that struggled, but ultimately found seeking God and following His will for their lives, put them back on the right path. From the beginning of time, man has dealt with the same issues and found the same answer; life is so much easier when we are obedient to God and abide in His word.

Surrender to Jesus Christ doesn't mean we lose our individuality or freedom. What we can lose is strife, sadness, turmoil, and darkness and replace them with peace, joy, contentment, and abundance. We don't have to struggle and live a roller-coaster life.

The answer to every question or struggle comes from the Living Word of God. Every word is the truth, and the Bible is the key to life and living it abundantly. When we truly learn what God's Word tells us, our outlook changes.

We are never alone. God hovers over His children, waiting patiently. All we have to do is invite Him in; He will take care of the rest.

Prologue

This book was written through the power of the Holy Spirit and in His name, Christ Jesus. He is my Lord, my Savior, my King. He is the light of the world.

Throughout the Bible, there are so many references to God's light. His very first words spoken to us and recorded in the book of Genesis are "Let there be light." God divided the light from darkness. (see Genesis 1: 3-4)

This was on the first day. On the third day he created the sun, the moon and the stars. This differentiated "God's light" from the "lights in the firmament." (see Genesis 1: 14-18)

When we accept Jesus as our Lord and Savior, we no longer walk in darkness but become God's light.

Heavenly Father, I pray for the reader, that the messages in this book will encourage them to make the greatest and most important decision of their life: Turning from darkness to light, through Christ Jesus.

For it is written:
"As I live, says the Lord, every knee shall bow to Me,
and every tongue shall confess to God"
(Romans 14:11; Isaiah 45:23, NKJV).

"Show Me the Way"
Styx—1990

Show me the way *I should go, for to you I lift up my soul. Rescue* **me** *from my enemies, O LORD, for I hide myself in you. Teach* **me** *to do your will, for you are my God; may your good Spirit lead* **me** *on level ground.*

—Psalms 143, NKJV

I found these lyrics from Styx's "Show Me the Way" during my research and was amazed by just how appropriate they are for what's going on in our world today. It is a perfect beginning for this book. Christ is there for us through all of our trials and tribulations, and He will *show us the way.*

Every night I say a prayer in the hope that there's a heaven

But every day I'm more confused as the saints turn into sinners

All the heroes and legends I knew as a child have fallen to idols of clay

And I feel this empty place inside, so afraid that I've lost my faith

Show me the way, show me the way

Take me tonight to the river

And wash my illusions away

Please, show me the way

And as I slowly drift to sleep, for a moment dreams are sacred

I close my eyes and know there's peace in a world so filled with hatred

Then I wake up each morning and turn on the news to find we've so far to go

And I keep on hoping for a sign, so afraid I just won't know

Show me the way, show me the way

Bring me tonight to the mountain

And take my confusion away

And show me the way

And if I see your light, should I believe

Tell me how will I know

Show me the way, show me the way

Take me tonight to the river
And wash my illusions away
Show me the way, show me the way
Give me the strength and the courage
To believe that I'll get there someday
And please show me the way
Every night I say a prayer in the hopes that there's a
heaven...

—Styx, "Show Me the Way"

Today I pray to my Father in Heaven. Please, show me the way!

Psalms 23: 4-5, NKJV

"Show me your ways, Lord, teach me your paths. Guide me in your truth and teach me, for you are God my Savior, and my hope is in you all day long."

3

There is a Season, Turn, Turn, Turn! (Pete Seeger, Lyrics Recorded in 1959)

To everything there is a season, A time for every purpose under heaven: A time to be born And a time to die; A time to plant, And a time to pluck what is planted; A time to kill, And a time to heal; A time to break down, And a time to build up; A time to weep, And a time to laugh; A time to mourn, And a time to dance; A time to cast away stones, And a time to gather stones; A time to embrace, And a time to refrain from embracing; A time to gain, And a time to lose; A time to keep, And a time to throw away; A time to tear, And a time to sew; A time to keep silence, And a time to speak; A time to love, And a time to hate; A time of war, And a time of peace.

—Ecclesiastes 3: 1-8, NKJV

The root word season (*epochi*) in the Greek language means time or for a time. We think of a season as being a long time. This is not what the Bible is referring to. In biblical terms, a season could be a day, a month, a year, or a lifetime. Regardless of how long a season lasts, change will come.

There was no time with God except when He came down to Earth, and Christ stepped into time for a season.

Scripture tells us there will be joy and sorrow, ups and downs, seasons we will rejoice, and seasons that we will mourn. God's children will endure suffering in certain times and seasons. When we face dark seasons in our lives, there *will* be light right around the corner. It is up to us to endure all seasons good or bad and hold on to the promises of God. He is with us at all times. We must learn to embrace everything God puts before us and acknowledge that He will get us through every season.

Sadness will turn to happiness, fear will turn to boldness, and loss will turn to gain. Regardless of our circumstances, our Heavenly Father uses all situations for the good of His Kingdom. We must have faith that God is always in control and will deliver us from every circumstance, making us better and stronger than before.

As I am writing this book, we are facing a pandemic, the coronavirus, and there is no answer as to when it might end. We are "sheltering in place," instructed to "keep our social distancing," and finding ourselves in a time when we are supposed to *refrain from embracing.*" We can find comfort that this season too shall pass, that God is with us always and better days are ahead.

Today, I pray for endurance. I accept there are seasons for everything and believe that nothing is too big for my Heavenly Father. I ask Father God to give me serenity and peace in times of trouble and will lean on Him when life seems too much to bear. I will be thankful for each season that He brings me and trust that He is sovereign—He sees and knows all. I surrender my life, my desires to take control of my situation or season. And when darkness surrounds me, I will seek *His* face, seek *His* light, and hold on to *His* promise that this too shall pass. I will thank *Him* for every season in my life.

1 Peter 5:6-9, NKJV

Therefore, humble yourselves under the mighty hand of God, that He may exalt you in due time, casting all your care upon Him, for He cares for you. Be sober, be vigilant; because your adversary the devil walks about like a roaring lion, seeking whom he may devour. Resist him, steadfast in the faith, knowing that the same sufferings are experienced by your brotherhood in the world.

Does Anybody Really Know What Time It Is?

The race is not to the swift, nor the battle to the strong, nor bread to the wise, nor riches to men of understanding, nor favor to men of skill; but time and chance happen to them all. For man also does not know his time; like fish taken in a cruel net, like birds caught in a snare, so the sons of men are snared in an evil time, when it falls suddenly upon them.

—Ecclesiastes 9:11-12, NKJV

Eternal life is very hard to comprehend. For those who do not believe that Christ died for us on the cross, there is only one life and one death here on Earth. It is a very frightening concept to believe that death is imminent and final.

The measurement of time was given to man to keep order in our lives. The average life span is around seventy-five years, during which we experience the "aging" of our bodies and, often, our minds. The question of age only applies to the bodies we dwell in while on this Earth. The great news is although our days here on Earth are short, and we will experience death of the flesh, our spirit lives on forever. When we accept salvation, the fear of dying goes away and gives us a clearer understanding of infinite time (God's time).

For our Father in Heaven, time is infinite; He does not exist in time. No one will know until we are able to ask Him how this works. For man, it is one of the wonders that we will only fully comprehend when we meet Him face to face.

It is confusing to reconcile what we've learned in school with the book of Genesis, which tells us how God created the universe. According to science, the earth is millions of years old, and yet scripture tells us that God created heaven and earth in six days. God's day is not the same as Man's day. One day for God is like a thousand years (see 2 Peter 3-8, NKJV) This helps with any doubt or confusion we have when dwelling on time.

Our comfort should lie in the fact that He did create all things, including the calendar for man to live by. He is infinite and all things are possible for our Heavenly Father.

Today, I thank you Father for giving me eternal life through the sacrifice of Your only begotten Son. For we know that once we become a follower of Jesus Christ, we will never perish, but have everlasting life. When I join You in heaven, I will understand that time is infinite.

1 John 2:17, NKJV

And the world is passing away, and the lust of it; but he who does the will of God abides forever.

2 Peter 3:8, NKJV

But do not forget this one thing dear friends; With the Lord a day is like a thousand years and a thousand years are like a day.

We Don't Know What Someone Else Is Going Through

Judge not, that you be not judged. For with what judgment you judge, you will be judged; and with the measure you use, it will be measured back to you. And why do you look at the speck in your brother's eye, but do not consider the plank in your own eye? Or how can you say to your brother, "Let me remove the speck from your eye," and look, a plank is in your own eye? Hypocrite! First, remove the plank from your own eye, and then you will see clearly to remove the speck from your brother's eye."

—Matthew 7: 1-5, NKJV

Empathy is the ability to understand and share the feelings of others. When we encounter someone who is withdrawn, quiet, or rude, there is no way for us to know what they are going through, unless we ask. It is human nature to be offended, take it personally and respond in a negative way. The saying "don't judge someone until you walk a mile in their shoes" reminds us that we have no idea what is causing their behavior. As followers of Jesus Christ, we should approach the person with empathy and love. We can't be argumentative or defensive if we are living in Christ.

I am reminded of a story told by a minister many years ago. He was asked to speak at a large Christian seminar, and after he completed the sermon, he invited a group of people from the church to join him for dinner. Seated at the restaurant and ready for a celebratory meal, they had a waitress that appeared very rude and unfocused. She had no response to their cheerful greetings and throughout the meal was impatient, defensive, and delivered terrible service. It was so bad that the group complained to each other, and what started out as a very positive experience turned negative. Many of them suggested to the minister that he complain to management or leave her little or no tip.

The minister asked the rest of the group to meet him outside so he could settle the bill. He waited until the waitress came back to the table, then asked if something were bothering her and if he could pray with her. The woman immediately burst into tears and explained that she had lost her child the previous day. She couldn't afford to take even one day off to grieve her loss, because she needed money to cover the burial expenses. Filled with compassion, he prayed with her and then left a substantial tip.

Today, if someone offends me, I will not take it personally. If possible, I will ask this person if they are having a bad day or facing something challenging. I will offer to pray with them, if not pray *for* them. I don't know what someone else may be going through and will treat them with love and empathy. Through my Lord and Savior, I ask for the strength to never go on the defensive but be filled with compassion for my sisters and brothers.

Romans 12:15, NKJV

Rejoice with those who rejoice, and weep with those who weep.

Colossians 3:12, NKJV

So, as those who have been chosen of God, holy and beloved, put on a heart of compassion, kindness, humility, gentleness and patience.

When Darkness Falls

And he prayed that he might die...suddenly an angel touched him, and said to him, "Arise and eat."
—1 Kings 19: 4-5, NKJV

Elisha was overwhelmed with depression to the point he no longer wanted to live. He received a very short and simple command from Heaven, "arise and eat." It was a command from God, telling Elisha to stop feeling sorry for himself and go on with life.

Man is prone to depression, and all of us will face it during our lifetime. It is an overwhelming feeling where even the simplest things we do become difficult. Getting out of bed, staying nourished, and going about our daily routines feel like impossible tasks.

We live in a time when there is a pill for everything to mask or hide our pain. Certainly, there are those who need certain medicines, including those with depression. However, there is a grave danger in masking our feelings. Without depression, we would never feel happiness or elation.

Life itself serves up things that will depress us: death, loss of a job, divorce, or money troubles. If we dwell on depression, it will overcome our entire being. This is when we must lift ourselves up, put one foot in front of the other, and follow Jesus.

Inspiration is everywhere we look, and God is in everything we do. When we are feeling depressed, it is time to focus on His miracles all around us—a warm breeze, an animal, a small child, a roof over our heads, or food in the refrigerator. When we focus on the simplest, most natural things, we find Jesus is with us. Finding inspiration and giving thanks will battle our depression, and the more we seek God, the quicker it will dissipate. It is up to each of us to "arise and eat."

Today, when I start to feel depressed, let me not lie down and hide, but let me "arise and eat." I will start by accomplishing the simple things, while seeing God in all that is around me. The Spirit of God is everywhere, and I will find inspiration and strength in Him. When I seek Him, my mood is immediately lifted!

Philippians 4:8, NKJV

Finally, brethren, whatever things are true, whatever things are noble, whatever things are just, whatever things are pure, whatever things are lovely, whatever things are of good report, if there is any virtue and if there is anything praiseworthy—meditate on these things.

Psalms 42:11, NKJV

Why are you cast down, O my soul? And why are you disquieted within me? Hope in God; For I shall yet praise Him. The help of my countenance and my God.

What Should I Pray?

*But seek first the kingdom of God and His righteousness,
and all these things shall be added to you.*
—Matthew 6:33, NKJV

First and foremost, when praying, we should start by giving thanks to our Heavenly Father. Even in times of trials and tribulations, we need to praise and worship Him. In fact, there are times when we may be overloaded with troubles, worries, and doubts, and we can feel too overwhelmed to pray. This is the best time to just say, "Thank you, Father! Thank you, Jesus!" It is amazing how quickly our troubles fade away when we are thankful.

After honoring God with thanksgiving, we bring our petitions before Him. Then we ask that His will be done. For many things that we ask outside of His will are not good for us. Our Father sees and knows if our prayers will bless or curse us, and we need to be thankful for both answered and unanswered prayers.

Finally, we must pray, as well as be anxious for nothing. For Jesus instructs us not to worry about what we will eat, where we will sleep, or if we will have clothes to wear; our Father knows all these things and will provide us everything we need.

There may be times we pray continually for a specific request without answer. Our prayers are answered not only according to His will, but also in His time. Time will also reveal the reason for unanswered prayers. Either way, we should be thankful. If we are always seeking God's kingdom, our lives will be blessed.

The most important thing as followers of Jesus Christ is that we take time each day to pray. In times when our minds are racing and we are struggling with what to say, Jesus gives us the Lord's prayer. It's a great way to give Him honor, request our needs be met, and keep the devil away!

Today, if I am struggling with what to pray, I will say the Lord's prayer. I will say thank you to my Father and Jesus for all things. Any troubles or worries on my heart, I give to my loving Father in Heaven. I ask for patience to wait on Him, and I find peace in the knowledge that He answers all prayers according to His will and time.

Mathew 6: 9-1, NKVJ

"Our Father in Heaven, Hallowed by Your name. Your kingdom come, your will be done, on earth as it is in Heaven. Give us this day our daily bread, and forgive us our debts, as we forgive our debtors. And do not lead us into temptation, but deliver us from the evil one, for Yours is the kingdom and the power and the glory forever. Amen."

Philippians 4:6, NKJV

"Be anxious for nothing, but in everything by prayer and supplication, with thanksgiving, let your requests be made known to God..."

A Secret Place

"But you, when you pray, go into your room, and when you have shut your door, pray to your Father who is in the secret place; and your Father who sees in secret will reward you openly."

—Matthew 6:6, NKJV

There are times when we should pray with others, especially when petitioning for a miracle like healing. In fact, Jesus tells us that when two or more are gathered together in His name, He will be in the midst.

However, for the most part, prayer is our private time to share with our Father. It is in these private moments with Him that our relationship grows, and He will speak to us. This may be what Jesus means when He refers to "the secret place." It is a time we are alone with our Father and stripped away are all the outside noises and deterrents that keep us from focusing on Him.

Prayer is more than just petitions of what we need or want, but a private conversation, when we have His undivided attention. It works best when we have a dedicated time each day for prayer, like a workout schedule. When we physically start to exercise, the endorphins start building. As we continue the routine, we find the stamina needed to exercise, which, once stimulated, it becomes something we look forward to.

We can start with a few minutes a day in prayer and start exercising our spirit. Our desire to pray will grow, and before we know it, our prayer time will become longer and more frequent.

There is no need for formality or religious chants, but rather prayer should be like talking to our earthly fathers. Ultimately, our prayer time will be like breathing, part of our very being, and something we don't want to live without.

We may pray in the shower or during our drive to and from work. As we continue to grow in faith, prayer becomes second nature—an ongoing conversation with our Father. Soon, we will find ourselves in constant prayer and communication with Him, leading to a burden free life and total serenity.

Today, I am so thankful to have a Heavenly Father ready to hear my prayers anytime and from anywhere! I will call on Him in calm or tumultuous times, knowing that He is always there. I am ready to commit to constant conversation with Him until the time that it becomes second nature to me. I will listen to what He tells me and accept His guidance for my life.

Jeremiah 29: 12-13, NKJV

Then you will call upon Me and go and pray to Me, and I will listen to you. And you will seek Me and find Me, when you search for Me with all your heart.

James 5:16, NKJV

The effective, fervent prayer of a righteous man avails much.

The Loss of Billy Graham—the Greatest Evangelist of Our Time

Being a Christian is more than just an instantaneous conversion; it is like a daily process whereby you grow to be more and more like Christ.

—Billy Graham, "A Daily Process," Devotional

While I was writing this book in 2018, Billy Graham, the world's greatest and most iconic evangelist, went to be with our Lord. His words about his death were, "Do not be sad for me when I am gone, for all I am doing is changing houses!"

The world met Billy Graham in 1946 when William Randolph Hearst, media mogul, issued a two-word directive to all his publications. "Puff Graham" was the mandate Hearst issued, and quickly other newspapers and news magazines descended on Dr. Graham's rallies. There were an estimated 350,000 attendees at the Los Angeles crusade tent, where thousands of people came to Christ. The rest, as they say, is history; that same year, Graham made his first trip overseas and continued preaching throughout the United States and Europe.

It was hard not to watch and listen to Billy Graham. He was mesmerizing: with movie star looks, a strong, compelling voice, a charmingly soft Southern accent, and an amazing stage presence. His message was as simple as it was powerful: Our lives on earth are short. Soon enough, each of us will die. Do we want to go to heaven? Then we must give our life to Christ. We must accept Him as our Lord and Savior and enter into a personal relationship with Him. Jesus is lovingly extending His hand to us. Will we take it? Referring to Scripture, Billy Graham would say, "Now is the accepted time; today is the day of salvation. This is the hour of decision." He would then give an alter call, and during his lifetime, Graham saved hundreds of thousands of souls.

The evangelical Graham was a moral conservative and civil rights liberal. At a crusade in 1953, he threatened to leave unless the organizers removed ropes, they had put in place to segregate the races. He befriended Martin Luther King Jr., who accepted Graham's invitation to preach at one of his New York City crusades, and even posted bail for King when he was arrested in Albany, Georgia. Graham viewed integration less as a constitutional issue than as a religious imperative. He insisted that segregation was unscriptural, and that blacks and whites were equal "at the foot of the cross."

There is so much more that could be written about the greatest evangelist of our time, and I have no doubt that his message will continue to affect many generations to come. He was a true man of God that taught the very message of Jesus Christ: repent and be saved.

Today, I celebrate the life of Billy Graham and look forward to our meeting someday when I too change houses. I too will spread the gospel of Jesus Christ and the message to repent and seek salvation. A movement can start with me, and I accept the challenge. Father give me the strength and persistence needed to tell everyone I meet the time is now and the day of judgement is near. Now is the day of salvation!

1 John 1:9, NKJV

If we confess our sins, he is faithful and just and will forgive us our sins and purify us from all unrighteousness.

Romans 13:11, NKJV

And do this knowing the time, that now it is high time to awake out of sleep; for now, our salvation is nearer than when we first believed.

Galatians 4: 1-7, NKJV

Now I say that the heir, as long as he is a child, does not differ at all from a slave, though he is master of all, but is under guardians and stewards until the time appointed by the father. Even so we, when we were children, were in bondage under the elements of the world. But when the fullness of the time had come, God sent forth His son, born of a woman, born under the law, to redeem those who were under the law, that we might receive the adoption as sons. And because you are sons, God has sent forth the Spirit of His Son into your hearts, crying out, "Abba Father." Therefore, you are no longer a slave but a son, and if a son, then an heir of God through Christ.

Stress'll Kill Ya!

Many are the afflictions of the righteous. But the Lord delivers him out of them all.

—Psalms 34:19, NKJV

In a medical or biological context, stress is a physical, mental, or emotional factor that causes bodily or mental tension. The causes of stress can be uncertainty, pressure, strain, worry, or fear. It manifests itself into chronic fatigue, anger, and feelings of helplessness. Stress has been directly related to physical ailments, including headaches, migraines, high blood pressure, fatigue, heart disease, and cancer.

Stress comes from an outside source; it is an adverse reaction to any change that requires an adjustment or response and affects both believers and non-believers. The difference is a believer has the word of God and our faith brings the manifestation of peace. The word allows us to overcome our troubles and afflictions. We should view stress as the enemy and take it captive through Scripture. We can rest in our Father's promise to deliver us from evil and refuse to be stressed out. We can find assurance and rest in the fact that Christ defeated our afflictions, troubles, and fears at the cross.

Trouble does not mean we are in distress. When trouble shows up, we need to go to the Word, see what it tells us, and be confident that "Our worries are handled!!" We should immediately open our mouths and thank God for every affliction we face and His deliverance from them.

Whatever we are facing, God promises us victory. We can conquer anything through the blood of Christ. The Word tells us we are going to face afflictions and troubles, but our Heavenly Father promises not just to deliver us through one of them or a few of them. He promises to deliver us through all of them!

Today, when facing trouble or affliction, I will not allow myself to be stressed out about it. I will go to the Word of God to find relief and delivery. There's a scripture for all of our troubles. I refuse to give hold to the enemy, worry about my situation, or get caught in his "net." ("Surely in vain the net is spread, In the sight of any bird," Proverbs 1:17, NKJV.) I will thank Jesus for His sacrifice on the cross, and when trouble comes, I will proclaim His blood covers me with peace and victory.

John 14:1, NKJV

Let not your heart be troubled; you believe in God, believe also in Me.

2 Corinthians 4:8-10, NKJV

We are hard-pressed on every side, yet not crushed; we are perplexed, but not in despair; persecuted, but not forsaken; struck down but not destroyed—always carrying about in the body the dying of the Lord Jesus, that the life of Jesus also may be manifested in our body.

John 16: 33, NKJV

These things I have spoken to you, that in Me you may have peace. In the world you will have tribulation; but be of good cheer, I have overcome the world.

Mind Your Own Business!

For I fear lest, when I come, I shall not find you such as I wish, and that I shall be found by you such as you do not wish; lest there be contentions, jealousies, outburst of wrath, selfish ambitions, backbitings, whisperings, conceits, tumults.

—2 Corinthians 12:20, NKJV

Gossip is evil. It's really as simple as that. In Paul's letter to the Corinthians, he is addressing the church who has fallen into sin, having turned against themselves and causing turmoil and descent. Instead of looking within to measure their own strength or weakness in following Christ, they were attacking each other. Paul makes very clear later in the chapter that this type of behavior "disqualifies" them from being true Christians.

When we allow ourselves to talk about other people, it corrupts our minds, bodies, and souls from the simplicity of Christ and everything He stands for. It grieves the Holy Spirit. Gossip is most often rooted in jealousy, and when you repeat what a third party has said about someone, it is slander. Once a rumor is started, there is a snowball effect. Once spread, it gets further and further away from the truth. As Christians, we must avoid this temptation. If we are rooted in Christ and truly believe in loving all others, we will stop engaging in this type of behavior. We must learn to walk away when we see others causing strife and contention, especially when it's at someone else's expense. It is our duty, as followers of Jesus Christ, to tell them you refuse to be involved, and whenever possible, through love and Scripture, attempt to correct their errored ways.

Most importantly, if we witness someone being attacked, especially behind his or her back, we should reach out directly to the person being harmed to befriend and support them. Gossip, contention, or jealousy not only hurts the target, but also our own hearts. These sinful acts do nothing but draw us closer to the enemy and farther away from God.

Today, I will avoid the temptation of gossip. If I see another person under attack, Father, please give me the strength and courage to correct the wrongdoings and show unconditional love to them. I will take no part in corruption, backstabbing, or spreading stories. If I am the one under attack, I will forgive those attacking me. I will show everyone the love of Christ that is in my heart and walk away from those who choose to spread hate.

Leviticus 9:16, NKJV

You shall not go about as a talebearer among your people; nor shall you take a stand against the life of your neighbor: I am the Lord.

Ephesians 4: 29-32, NKJV

Let no corrupt word proceed out of your mouth, but what is good for necessary edification, that it may impart grace to the hearers. And do not grieve the Holy Spirit of God, by whom you were sealed for the day of redemption. Let all bitterness, wrath, anger, clamor, and evil speaking be put away from you, with all malice. And be kind to one another, tenderhearted, forgiving one another, even as God in Christ forgave you.

James 1:26, NKJV

If anyone among you thinks he is religious and does not bridle his tongue but deceives his own heart, this one's religion is useless.

How Did I Get Here?

I will arise and go to my father and will say to him, "Father, I have sinned against heaven and before you, and I am no longer worthy to be called your son, make me like one of your hired servants.
—Luke 15:18-19, NKJV

When we walk away from God, we have no anchor in our life. God intends for us stay connected. When we make a decision to depart from Him, our lives will surely take a wrong turn. It does not matter if we have all the money in the world or have nothing at all. If we turn away from our Heavenly Father, it costs us everything. When we start wanting the wrong things in life, the Devil steps in and says, "Follow me!" He promises us a life without restraints, no rules or consequences. This is a *lie!* If we turn from God, there is a dire consequence, which is eternal damnation.

We may start off with slight discontent, and sooner than later find ourselves in a great state of misery, wondering, "How did I get here?" Dissolution turns to despair, and we become lost, away from the only thing that brings us satisfaction, peace, and joy: our Heavenly Father.

When in this state of misery, we can look back and see the first step, the very point in our life that we turned away from God, then step by step how we lost our way. It is when we are as low as we can get that we finally call out to God and plead with Him to bring us back into a state of grace.

This is similar to the story of the prodigal son, who took and blew his inheritance and found himself working in a hog pen hungry, broke, and alone. He made the decision to leave, go home, and plead with his father to take him back as a servant, admitting he was unworthy to be called his son. The son was ready and willing to repent and beg for forgiveness, accepting anything that his father might offer. But before he could get to his father's house, the father ran to him, opened his arms, welcomed him home as his son, and gave him a second chance! The father celebrated his return, and the son was back to his place in life.

This is the road to redemption that we too must follow. We must repent, turn back, pray for forgiveness, and then sit back and watch what God will do to straighten our paths. He is always willing to bring us back into his fold with loving arms and grace. Wherever we are, it's never too late. Our Heavenly Father is a loving and forgiving God, ready to receive us if we only ask. He will forgive our transgressions and sins. All we have to do is ask with a humble heart, and He will restore us. He is always ready to hear us and bring us home into His loving and righteous hands. We are always just one prayer away from total redemption!

Today, I am in a state of misery, lost and wondering, *"How did I get here?"* I cry out to You, Father, and ask You in the name of Jesus to please here my prayer:

Heavenly Father, I have sinned against You and disobeyed You. Miserably lost, I ask You to forgive me of my sins; not because I am worthy but because Jesus gave His life in Calvary to bear my sins and wash me with His blood. Father, I have messed up my life and broken the lives of others through my actions and disobedience. I ask you to give me a new beginning in the name of Jesus Christ.

Pray this prayer and watch what happens! Your burdens will be lifted, your life complete, and you will immediately feel the joy and love of God's grace and redemption.

James 4:17, NKJV

Therefore, to him who knows to do good and does not do it, to him it is sin.

Luke 15: 20-24, NKJV

And he arose and came to his father. But when he was still a great way off, his father saw him and had compassion, and ran and fell on his neck and kissed him. But the father said to his servants, "Bring out the best robe and put it on him and put a ring on his hand and sandals on his feet. And bring the fatted calf here and kill it and let us eat and be merry; for this my son was dead and is alive again; he was lost and is found." And they began to be merry.

Ezekiel 34:12, NKJV

"As a shepherd seeks out his flock on the day he is among his scattered sheep, so will I seek out My sheep and deliver them from all the places where they were scattered on a cloudy and dark day."

Luke 15:7, NKJV

"I say to you that likewise there will be more joy in heaven over one sinner who repents than over ninety-nine just persons who need no repentance."

There's NOTHING to Worry About!

And do not seek what you should eat or what you should drink, nor have an anxious mind. For all these things the nations of the world seek after, and your Father knows that you need these things.

—Luke 12:29-30, NKJV

It is human nature when we are facing instability and uncertain times for our minds to immediately go to the worst-case scenarios. We start focusing on all the "what ifs" and try to work out solutions to what might happen. This does nothing but cause great anxiety and stress. Worry will cause lack of sleep and concentration; if continued, it will manifest itself into mental and physical illnesses.

When worry consumes us, we allow Satan to take a stronghold on our emotions, and it gives him access to our souls. We drive ourselves crazy on thoughts of how we will overcome the inevitable. In reality, all we are doing is creating problems that do not exist, stealing our joy, and weakening our spirit. Most of what we spend our time worrying about never even happens.

Focusing on the "what ifs" causes fear, and that is one of the enemy's most popular weapons. Fear can overwhelm us with a thick shadow of darkness, controlling our every move and decision. We must surrender ourselves, dwell on the power of God, and be confident in His promises. Surrender gives way to serenity, weakness gives way to strength, meekness gives way to power, and submission gives way to victory!

Our lives are but a fleeting moment, and we must see that our Father in Heaven has been in control from before we were born and will stay in control until we take our last breath. Anxiety is opposed to trust in God, and only when we release it, do we find ultimate peace and a worry-free life. When we finally accept that He is in control, we will find a peace that exceeds all understanding, a joy that is supernatural, and a calm over our lives that we have never experienced. He surrounds us with his protection and will always meet our needs.

Today, I lay down my burdens on the cross. I surrender all of my worries and anxieties to You and wait for Your serenity to fill my mind, body, and soul. I pray that all of my needs and those of my loved ones are provided and give thanks to the Father. I will read Your words of life and truth. Soaking them in, over and over, and praying them out loud until they become so familiar, they replace negative thoughts and dissipate all of my worries.

Luke 12:22-23, NKJV

Then he said to His disciples, "Therefore I say to you, do not worry about your life, what you will eat; nor about the body, what you will put on. Life is more than food, and the body is more than clothing."

Luke 12: 25-26, NKJV

"And which of you by worrying can add one cubit to his stature? If you then are not able to do the least, why are you anxious for the rest?"

Is My Own House in Order?

And if it seems evil to you to serve the Lord, choose for your-
selves this day whom you will serve, whether the gods which
your fathers served that were on the other side of the river, or
the gods of the Amorites, in whose land you dwell. But as for
me and my house, we will serve the Lord.

—Joshua 24:15, NKJV

The life of King David exemplifies not only Man's struggle with the flesh, but the depth of God's love for His children and His willingness to forgive even the most egregious sins. When studying the book of Psalms, we can see David's reliance on God. He battles with sin and constantly cries for the Lord's help. We know that David was a great king, and he was favored by God and used that favor to conquer many enemies and gain incredible power and riches. Yet through all

God blessed him with, David struggled to keep his own house in order.

Although he was known to be the wisest of men, he committed the greatest of sins, including coveting another man's wife. He committed adultery, murder, and betrayed one of his closest and most loyal servants. Unable to truly accept what he had done, David attempted to sweep his sins under the rug. Because he turned from God in shame, he started losing control of his kingdom. Only when his greatest advisor came to him did he finally recognize the damage and depths of his sin. Although he prayed for forgiveness and protection over his family, it was too late, and God took the son he'd had with Bathsheba and allowed another son to turn against him and threaten his kingdom. One of his sons raped his daughter, and then he lost another son. In totality, five lives in the kingdom were shattered because of David's sin.

Finally, broken and feeling abandoned, he turned back to his Heavenly Father and repented. Only when King David's house was back in order, did he once again find favor with God. He and Bathsheba were blessed with another son who became the richest, most powerful king in history. The most amazing blessing that God showed David was that Jesus Christ would descend directly from his house.

So, what should we take away from the story of King David? First, we should take inventory of our own house and make sure it is in order. Ask ourselves:

"Does my house serve the Lord?"

"Am I providing a good example for my children by living a sanctified life?"

"Are my children followers of Christ?"

"Is there sin in my life blocking my blessings and jeopardizing the ones that I love?"

Today, I will take inventory of my house, and make sure "It is in order." If there is sin, I will repent. If there is affliction or trouble, I will pray for deliverance. I claim this day that, for me and my house, we will serve the Lord!

Deuteronomy 11:13-15, NKJV

And it shall be that if you earnestly obey My commandments to which I command you today, to love the Lord your God and serve Him with all your heart and with all your soul, then I will give you the rain for your land in its season, the early rain and the latter rain, that you may gather in your grain, your new wine, and your oil. And I will send grass in your fields for your livestock, that you may eat and be filled.

Psalms 2:11, NKJV

Serve the Lord with fear and rejoice with trembling.

Will I Hear "Job Well Done"?

His lord said unto him, "Well done, good and faithful servant: you have been faithful over a few things, I will make you ruler over many things: enter into the joy of your lord."

—Matthew 25:23, NKJV

The story of the Good Samaritan is known by believers and non-believers throughout the world. For the non-believers, it is more of a fable about helping your neighbor and being a good person. For the believer, it should resonate much deeper, and we need to see exactly what Jesus is teaching us in this parable. The Good Samaritan teaches us that we must open our eyes, hearts, hands, and possessions. That we must go above and beyond what others would do to help our brothers and sisters, regardless of their color, religion, or social status.

The Samaritan could have easily done what the two before him had done and look the other way. He could have justified his actions by saying to himself, "I can't help this man, or he's not my problem, *but I'll pray for him!*" Instead, the Good Samaritan chose to help to the best of his ability and follow through until the injured man was fully healed. Although the situation must have looked overwhelming and helpless, he gave everything within his means and abilities to help a total stranger in need.

If I could only use one word that causes Christians to fall short of the glory of God, it would be *self-centeredness.* This is especially true for Westerners, who have been brought up with a sense of entitlement. When we put ourselves first, over God and others, we are basically saying "I am the most important," "my needs I put before everyone else," and "I have the power over my life." Our prayers become focused on what we need and want, always bargaining and pleading with God for more. We allow ourselves to become entangled in the flesh, losing sight of the spirit, ultimately isolating ourselves from our Heavenly Father. This leads us to feelings of total discontentment as we continue to seek more. Being self-centered causes us to fall off the path in our walk with Christ. This is why Jesus tells us it is so difficult for a rich man to enter the gates of Heaven, and we cannot serve two masters. If our focus is on gathering riches and power here on Earth, then we are not doing what is necessary to live a sanctified life and secure our place in Heaven.

I am not saying that we need to be poor to follow Jesus or give everything away to be considered a Christian. Quite the contrary, God wants us to have a full and rich life, as well as enjoy the fruits of our labor and be happy. But to whom much is given, much is required. We must never forget that everything we have is given to us by *Him*, that we are *His* stewards, and whether we have very little or an abundance, it is our duty as Christians to remember that everything we have belongs to God. We must be faithful to *Him* first and foremost.

We must ask ourselves this question: "Am I willing to accept all of God's blessings, but refuse to help (share with) others?" Our desire to serve Him must supersede the desires of our flesh, and then and only then will our Lord tell us, "Job well done, my good and faithful servant!"

Today, I will open my eyes and see those who are in need and suffering. I will open my heart, identify them, and acknowledge my power to help them. I will open my hands and let the Lord guide me. I will open my possessions, recognizing all that I have is from God, and joyfully give to those who have less and need help. I declare the Lord my God is first and foremost in my life, I am a sheep, and He is the Shepherd. I give Him thanks for all that I have and for enabling me to give to others. I will live a true life as a follower of Jesus Christ, who teaches me that giving and assisting my brothers and sisters are the keys to living a sanctified life. I will not walk away or ignore those who are suffering. And I pledge to serve Him all the days of my life!

1 Timothy 6:9-10, NKJV

But those who desire to be rich fall into temptation and a snare, and into many foolish and harmful lusts which drown men in destruction and perdition. For the love of money is a root of all kinds of evil, for which some have strayed from the faith in their greediness and pierced themselves through with many sorrows.

1 Timothy 6:18-19, NKJV

Let them do good, that they be rich in good works, ready to give, willing to share, storing up for themselves a good foundation for the time to come, that they may lay hold on eternal life.

Choose Life Over Death, Blessing Over Cursing!!!

The LORD is slow to anger, abounding in love and forgiving sin and rebellion. Yet he does not leave the guilty unpunished; he punishes the children for the sin of the parents to the third and fourth generation.

—Numbers 14:18, NKJV

The life of Joseph is a perfect portrayal of breaking a generational curse. In his lineage were great betrayals against family and God. Joseph was betrayed by his brothers, who were jealous and envious for he was his father's favorite son. His brothers left him for dead and sentenced him to a life of slavery and bondage. However, Joseph realized that what his brothers meant for evil, God meant for good, as he became one of the most powerful rulers in Egypt.

Joseph had years in which anger and resentment could have festered, but when he finally met his brothers, his heart was full of love and forgiveness. In a position to have easily caused them much pain and suffering, including death, he chose to do just the opposite and welcomed them back with open arms and a heart full of love.

A generational curse is a real thing. It could be abuse, betrayal, divorce, addiction, depression, money issues, and anything that has a supernatural stronghold that has caused suffering throughout generations. Whatever this curse may be, it is something we not only must identify but break. If we fail to deal with the problem (curse), then it will pass to our children and our children's children. We will send them into the world unable to live joyous or satisfying lives; they will miss lives full of blessings. Their ability to live peaceful lives will be blocked by ancestral sin.

All of us pray that our children will live a sanctified life, but that will never be obtained without breaking the family curse. Literally, whatever failures, problems, obstacles, pain, or heartache that we have inherited becomes theirs.

So, what do we do to avoid hurting our loved ones in this way? It starts by taking inventory of our lives, as well as those of our parents and grandparents, to identify the issue(s). Then we must fully accept and acknowledge the problem and how it has affected our family for generations. Once acknowledged, we must then do whatever it takes to change and break the curse. Most often, there will damage control with your loved ones, and depending how severe, it may be changed through prayer and forgiveness. More serious matters may take professional guidance and Christian counseling. It starts by asking our Heavenly Father not only to forgive us, but to forgive those whom He cursed, and then ask Him to help make the changes necessary to break the curse once and for all.

It is never too late, and even if our children are grown, we can guide them to stop the curse before it's passed on to another generation. I realize this is easier said than done, and when it happens there may be an overwhelming amount of guilt and grieving over the pain and suffering, we have afflicted on those we love the most. If there are siblings, I would encourage facing this challenge together, always remembering that Christ is there to guide and lead the way.

Regardless of how bad it may seem; our Father in Heaven has been waiting for the day when He can finally break our family's curse. He is ready to forgive all generations and to make a new covenant with all future generations. We will literally be breaking the chains that have bound our family for years.

Today, I will stop the suffering. I declare that in this generation, my family curse is broken. Whatever it takes to mend the pain, be forgiven of the sin, and clear the future for coming generations, I am ready to do. Father, strengthen me, guide me, and lead me. Show me the way, and I will follow your lead. Release these chains that have bound my family and set us free! The curse stops with me. It will not pass to my children or my children's children. *I pray for direction as I put on the armor of God which will protect me as I stand against and dispel all the evil and negative forces around my family.* I ask my Father for a new covenant that will bless all future generations from now to eternity. I choose life over death, blessing over cursing!

Genesis 50:18-21, NKJV

Then his brothers also went and fell down before his face, and they said, "Behold, we are your servants." Joseph said to them, "Do not be afraid, for am I in the place of God? But as for you, you meant evil against me; but God meant it for good, in order to bring it about as it is this day, to save many people alive. Now therefore, do not be afraid; I will provide for you and your little ones." And he comforted them and spoke kindly to them.

Deuteronomy 30:10, NKJV

Call heaven and earth as witnesses against you today that I have set before you life and death, blessing and cursing. So, choose life, so that you and your descendants may live.

God's Provisions for
His Children

*And my God shall supply all your need according to His
riches in glory by Christ Jesus.*
                                        —Philippians 4:19, NKJV

The story of Noah's Arc is known to most of the world.
Thought of more like a fable, a children's book, and often the theme of nurseries, very few people understand
the story is true. During the time of Noah, the world
had become very wicked, inhabited by giants who had
been procreated from fallen angels intermingling with
humans. The Lord was grieved and decided to destroy
what He had created by a great flood. However, Noah
and his family were *righteous* and found grace in the
eyes of the Lord. Knowing that Noah was an obedient
servant, God instructed him to build the arc. For one
year, they were ridiculed and taunted for building this
huge ship in the middle of the dessert. But Noah did

what God told him to do. He filled the ship with each kind of animal and at the end of the year, he gathered his family, then boarded and sealed the vessel.

It is unfathomable to think of what happened next, as the heavens opened to torrential rainfall. Noah and his family would have literally watched as the rain covered the earth. The people and animals were going up to the highest ground and crying out for help. It would've taken weeks for such a huge ship to actually start floating, and people would've been beating on the door, pleading for their lives and begging for their children's lives.

After forty days and forty nights, the rain stopped. It was close to one year when the water finally started to subside. Approximately three months later, the earth dried, and Noah, his family, and all of the animals were able to leave the arc. God gave Noah and his family dominion over the animals and the plants of the earth so that they would always have food and shelter. Then He instructed them to "go forth and multiply" (see Genesis 7- 8, NKVJ). God put a rainbow in the sky and told Noah that it was sign of His promise that He would never again cause a great flood.

The story of Noah and the flood is only three chapters in the book of Genesis but is one of the most powerful stories in the Bible. There are three things we can take away from this story. First is God's provision of protection against evil. Second is the provision of shelter and food, and His promise to always provide for us. Third is the promise of eternal life and love.

Regardless of how bad the world looks or how dark the days seem, He will never leave us, He will always provide for us, and we can rest in His promise of blessings and eternal life. We must also recognize that in the time of the final reckoning, He will protect us as He protected Noah and his family.

This story also shows the genuine love God has for this world and His children, and how wickedness and sin break His heart. This is something I think is really important for us to understand. When we sin against God, it grieves Him, and that should be enough to motivate us to never sin. God will not tolerate evil (although it is abounding in this fallen world,) nor allow Satan to gain total control. There will be a day, a *FINAL* day, when God defeats the devil once and for all. There will be total peace on earth. Good will prevail, and we all will live in paradise, worshiping our Heavenly Father.

Today looks really dark, and I feel surrounded by evil and wickedness. Everywhere I look, there is bad news and sin, and it seems like the devil is taking control. I am frightened for my future—will there be food and shelter? But I know that my Father in Heaven sees me and will never leave me. I can rest in His promise of provisions for all of His children. I find peace in the knowledge that evil *will* be defeated and good *will* prevail.

Genesis 6:4, NKJV

There were giants on the earth in those days, and also afterward, when the sons of God came into the daughters of men and they bore children to them."

Genesis 9:12-13, NKJV

And God said, "This is the sign of the covenant which I make between Me and you, and every living creature that is with you, for perpetual generations; I set My rainbow in the cloud, and it shall be for the sign of the covenant between Me and the earth.

Matthew 6:33, NKJV

But seek first the kingdom of God and His righteousness and all these things shall be added to you.

L-O-V-E—LOVE!!!!

L – I am the **L**ord your God. I give you **L**ife. I am the **L**iving God.

O – **O**pen your eyes. **O**pen you ears. **O**pen your heart. I will watch **O**ver you. I am your **O**nly God.

V – I am the **V**ine. I give you **V**ictory, **V**indicate you and seek **V**engeance against your enemies.

E – I am **E**verlasting, **E**xtraordinary, and **E**normous.

And now these three remain: faith, hope and love. But the greatest of these is love.
—1 Corinthians 13:13, NKJV

There is no greater gift than the love from our Father in Heaven! Because He Loved us so much, He allowed His only Son to go to the cross and bear the sins of the world. Jesus tells us that above all, we should love the Lord our God, one another, our neighbor, and even our enemies. If not for (His) love, we would have nothing. Love is what the world needs today.

Hatred surrounds us, and everywhere we look or turn there are hate crimes and hate groups. Our political arena is full of hatred with lines being drawn on both sides. Not only do other countries hate America, but many of our *own citizens* hate America! There is no middle; it's left or right; neutrality no longer exists; and we are becoming polarized.

Christians are hated around the world and blamed for everything that goes wrong. Civility is becoming a thing of the past, and "right fighters" run rampant, spewing words of deceit, hatred, and violence. We struggle to know what is true, what is good, and can no longer rely on people to tell the truth. The media, fueled with hatred, goes against everything that is ethical, making up lies to support their positions.

We have only *one* defense against hate, and that is *love!* When Jesus told us to love our enemies, He knew what was coming and could see these times happening. He was able to foresee that Christians would feel defenseless, hopeless, and defeated by darkness.

We cannot battle evil (the enemy) with hatred in our own hearts, but we can fight darkness with light. Light is love, and love is good, and our love must be stronger than ever to defeat the enemy who spreads all of his venom. When we become defensive, hurt or angry, then Satan wins. We must stand strong and focused and remove all hatred from our hearts. We must pray constantly, ask God to remove any negative thoughts or feelings, surrender our battles and vengeance against others, and plead for mercy and grace. This starts with each and every one of us, and we must share the love of Christ every chance we get. The time is now, for we truly are in a war against the principalities of darkness.

Today, I surrender any hatred, grief, anger, or negative feelings, and pray for my Heavenly Father to replace them with love. I promise to love my neighbor, co-worker, stranger, and especially my enemy. I refuse to listen to lies and haters, and I will focus on God's Word, reading Scripture, listening and watching Christian broadcasts, and attending worship services. I choose love and the Gospel over hatred and sin. I pledge my heart, body, mind, and soul to loving the Father, the Son, and the Holy Spirit. I ask my Father in Heaven to fill my heart with His love and help me spread it whenever and wherever I can. I will not be defeated by the enemy, take part in negative thoughts or actions, or give any credence to those spreading hate. I claim that I am a child of God, filled with His love, and I will share His message with all who will listen. *It starts with me!*

1 Corinthians 13: 1-3, NKJV

If I speak in the tongues of men or of angels, but do not have love, I am only a resounding gong or a clanging cymbal. If I have the gift of prophecy and can fathom all mysteries and all knowledge, and if I have a faith that can move mountains, but do not have love, I am nothing. If I give all I possess to the poor and give over my body to hardship that I may boast, but do not have love, it profits me nothing.

1 Corinthians 13:8, NKJV

Love never fails. But whether there are prophecies, they will fail; whether there are tongues, they will cease; whether there is knowledge, it will vanish away.

Two or More...

For where two or three are gathered together in my name, there am I in the midst of them.

—Matthew 18:20, NKJV

God loves when we spend time with Him privately in communion, building love, trust and an unbreakable bond. Our Heavenly Father desires for us to know Him intimately and identify Him as our protector and provider. Time alone with Him is the only way to build a solid foundation. There are times, however, that we need to join with one or more in prayer.

When two or more come together in prayer, not only does the dynamic change, but Jesus promises to join us and let our petitions be known to the Father. He will mediate so our prayers are answered. If two or more agree here on Earth, Jesus will be in the midst of them!

We may wonder why are we unable to get the results on our own that He promises when two or more pray together? The short answer is we can as long as our prayers align with God's will. However, our prayers become stronger and more effective when we join other believers.

We remove our own bias or lack of objectivity when we consult with another believer. We are looking for someone with our best interests in mind who will also tell us the truth. Our sisters and brothers in Christ will help us analyze our requests and determine that they align with God's Holy Word. Then, in agreement, we bring our prayers to Jesus, who will petition our Heavenly Father. This is when we can rest, assured that God will answer.

Think about the power we have to affect change and move mountains when we pray with other believers. Something that seems too overwhelming for one becomes totally possible for two or more. Together, we can start a movement, affect an outcome, and change the world!

Today, when wanting to make an important request to the Lord, I will ask one or more believers to join in my petition. What may seem impossible or overwhelming becomes possible through our union. Together we can make a difference in this world through prayer, knowing that Jesus Christ will be there with us

Matthew 18:19, NLJV

Again, I say unto you, that if two of you shall agree on earth as touching anything that they shall ask, it shall be done for them of my Father which is in Heaven.

*Jesus basically repeats the same point twice in this passage, which is interesting as He tended to do this in His teachings. When we see this in the Gospels, I believe we should really pay attention to the message!

"Don't Let the Sun Catch You Cryin'"

The night-time shadow disappears, and with them go all your tears, for the morning will bring joy, for every girl and boy, so don't let the sun catch you cryin'.

—Gerry and the Peacemakers,
"Don't Let the Sun Catch You Crying"

Light – (adjective, verb or noun) "something that makes vision possible, something that makes things visible...illuminates, ignites...a form of energy, bright, not heavy..."[1]

Dark – (adjective, very or noun) "devoid or partially devoid of light; arising from or showing evil traits or desires, dismal, gloomy, night or nightfall, to stop operating; to go off-line"[2] (Merriam-Webster Dictionary)

Be angry and do not sin; do not let the sun go down on your anger, nor give place to the devil.

—Ephesians 4:26-27, NKJV

There are many references throughout Scripture distinguishing light from dark. It is good versus evil, God versus Satan, and those who walk in the light versus those who walk in darkness. In our world, bad things happen at night; crime, drug and alcohol use, adultery, perversion, depression, anger, fear and loneliness. It is amazing how all these things seem to disappear in the morning light. It is in darkness, where many unhealthy and unacceptable secrets in a person's life flourish. This is because Satan operates at night and in darkness.

But what does this mean to Christians? First and foremost, we must recognize that God made day and night, light and darkness, a time to be awake and a time to sleep. Scripture tells us to walk in the light, God gives it light, let the light shine out of darkness, *and do not let the sun go down on your anger!* (see 1 John 1:7, NKJV)

God wants our sleep to be peaceful, therefore telling us not to go to bed angry. When we go to sleep angry or upset, we are subjecting these feelings to manifest in darkness and let the enemy take hold. Additionally, He is instructing us not to wake up angry or upset, but to start fresh, anew each day.

Loving darkness does not mix with following Jesus. As followers of Jesus Christ, it is up to us to expose evil and darkness by illuminating and making visible to others what is bad and wrong. Evil and darkness can spread just like a contagion, and it does devour people's souls. The enemy knows we are vulnerable in darkness and that we can't see things for what they really are under the covering of dark.

Darkness can't exist in the presence of God's light. Therefore, we must walk in light, meaning our thoughts, words, and actions must always align with Jesus. When we walk in this light it illuminates our being, and you can physically see this in believers and in those who are truly sanctified. There is literally a glow (illumination or light) on those who walk in the Holy Spirit and love the Lord. The distinction between light and dark is real. It is so important that we recognize this, and follow our Heavenly Father's instructions by reading, sharing, and practicing His word.

Today, I will not let anger, disappointment, mistakes, or any dark feelings upset me and linger through the night. Father, if I am walking in darkness, please shine your light on my transgressions. If encountering darkness or evil today, I will call on the strength of Jesus to help me expose and defeat the enemy by shining my light! For I know that the light of Christ is in me and therefore protects me against Satan and darkness. I cry out for mercy and profess any darkness that may be lurking in my heart. I will live and share the beauty of God's bright, cleansing light!

Psalms 97:11, NKJV

Light shines on the righteous and joy on the upright in heart.

Matthew 5:16, NKJV

Let your light so shine before men, that they may see your good works and glorify your Father in Heaven.

Acts 13:47, NKJV

"I have set you as a light to the Gentiles, that you should be for salvation to the ends of the earth."

Ephesians 5:8, NKJV

For at one time you were darkness, but now you are light in the Lord. Walk as children of light.

I've Got the Power...

For God has not given us a spirit of fear, but of power and of love and of a sound mind.

—2 Timothy 1:7, NKJV

Becoming spiritually strong is just like gaining physical strength. It takes commitment, practice, exercise, consistency, and time. In the beginning, when we first commit to working out, it is something we dread. It's easy to find excuses and tell ourselves, "I'll start tomorrow." Once we start and persevere, in about fourteen days of regular exercise, our endorphins increase, and our body starts craving the exercise. What was hard to do will become a habit and ultimately give us a happier and healthier life! It will become something we look forward to and wonder how we ever lived without.

The same is true with spiritual exercise which is prayer, meditation, and scriptural study. The enemy will put a thousand reasons and distractions in front of us to stop this from happening. He (Satan) knows that the more versed we become in God's word and the more we communicate with our Heavenly Father, the lower his chance is to separate us. This is the enemy's number one goal—to steal as many souls as he possibly can from God.

Just as exercise nourishes the body, God's Word nourishes our souls. The more we learn, the more we want to learn, and once the exercise becomes a habit, our minds will start to yearn for His word. The more we read and memorize, the stronger we become spiritually, and this strength becomes power. Power to fight the enemy, power to influence others to Christ, power to lead and protect our friends and family, power to be successful, and the power to know, *"I can do all things through Christ who strengthens me!"* (Philippians 4:13, NKVJ)

Today I will set up a schedule to start reading God's Word, meditating on His messages, and praying for wisdom and discernment. I am not going to set my expectations too high and cause myself to fail. I will start with five minutes each day, put down my phone or computer, and go to a quiet place where I will not be interrupted. And in the beginning, when the enemy tries to distract me, I will ask the Father to quiet my mind and shut down my racing thoughts and worries. Then I will open my Bible, read a short passage, and meditate on the meaning. I commit to continue each and every day, knowing that God's Word will empower and strengthen me. What starts as an exercise will soon become a habit and one that I look forward to every single day!

Joel 3:10, NKJV

Let the weak say, "I am strong."

Job 12:13, NKJV

With Him are wisdom and strength, he has counsel and understanding.

Philippians 4:13, NKJV

I can do all things through Christ who strengthens me.

Little Olé Me???

"My grace is sufficient for you, for my strength is made perfect in weakness."

—2 Corinthians 12:9 NKJV

The only thing necessary for the triumph of evil is that good men do nothing.

– Edmond Burke

When looking at the world and all of the bad things that are happening, it is natural to say to ourselves, "I am too small, weak and insufficient to make a change" or "What can I possibly do?" This gives way to feelings of insignificance, helplessness, and an overwhelming sense of hopelessness; we start focusing on our inability to affect change, right wrong, or fight evil. This is exactly what the enemy hopes for. If he can sway the masses to believe "there is nothing we can do, so we might as well do nothing," then he wins, and evil prevails. If Satan can influence the majority of believers to become stagnate, dormant, and apathetic like sheep, he will lead us to the slaughter.

We must ask ourselves, "Are we going to fight or forfeit, stand for good or fall for evil?" We only have two choices: to either do nothing or do something. It's time to call on Christ! He is our shepherd and will enable us to stand up and fight.

Okay, so this all sounds good, but *what* can we do? How can we make a difference and help defeat the enemy? Like Paul, we start by accepting our weakness and acknowledge our dependence on the Father, Son, and Holy Spirit. Then, we bring our petitions to the Father.

Prayer not only gives us strength but also guidance and wisdom. When we pray to God, we are bringing our petitions to the creator of the universe and there is no greater power!

We can reach out and touch someone through a donation, an act of kindness, or help someone who may be helpless. Pray for our leaders, lawmakers, and clergy who can and do affect change. Start a conversation with someone who doesn't know Christ and share what He has done in your life. Write and post something positive on Facebook or record a message and put it on YouTube. Instant message an old acquaintance or friend, ask how they're doing, and see if they need something you can provide. There are so many small things that each of us can do singularly and collectively to make positive changes for our world.

Today, I recognize my power to affect change. Rather than being overwhelmed by what I cannot do, I will recognize what I can do and *do it!* As I pray for guidance and understanding, the Holy Spirit will show me what to do to and how I can make a difference. I accept my weakness by receiving strength through the creator of the universe. I will ask other believers to join me in my cause. I will reach out to someone who doesn't know Christ and share my testimony. Most importantly, I choose to do something rather than nothing!

2 Corinthians 4:16-17, NKJV

Therefore, we do not lose heart. Even though our outward man is perishing, yet the inward man is being renewed day by day. For our light affliction, which is but for a moment, is working for us a far more exceeding and eternal weight of glory.

Romans 12:2, NKJV

And do not be conformed to this world, but be transformed by the renewing of your mind, that you may prove what is that good and acceptable and perfect will of God.

"There's No Unbelievers in a Foxhole!"

For whoever calls on the name of the Lord, shall be saved.
— Romans 10:13, NKJV

During WWI and WWII, the troops would dig deep holes right up on the enemy lines. If under fire, they could jump in these "foxholes" for protection. However, if the enemy was able to advance, the troops in the hole could also be sitting ducks. And so, on the brink of death or capture, it is said that many men who did not know the Lord came to Jesus in those last few seconds.

We can look at the most recent tragic event prior to the 2020 pandemic, which of course is 9/11—the attack on America. Shock and fear were palpable, and people rushed to the gas stations and grocery stores with anticipation of the end coming. *But* people also flocked to churches across the country and showed up for services in record numbers.

As I write this book, we are in the middle of the 2020 COVID-19 pandemic, and things are more uncertain now than they have ever been (in my lifetime). Although many churches are closed, the online search to seek God is growing exponentially. Once again, in a time of doom and gloom and feeling there is nowhere else to turn, people are turning to God in search of answers.

So *WHY* does it take a disaster or near-death experience for people to seek the Lord? When everything is going well in our lives, we have a false sense of independence and self-reliance. We desire to hold on to our independence until calamity hits or we are facing darkness and no longer feel in control. Only when we can't find the answer to our questions or figure out a plan to save ourselves and realize that our situation is so much greater than us, do we seek Him. It is when we are humbled, helpless, fearful, and see no natural way out of a terrible situation, that we recognize He is our only answer.

He is our plan and our salvation, our Protector, Creator, Rescuer. He is the ONE and ONLY true God. Our Father is faithful and true, a refuge and our hiding place. He loves us so much and waits patiently for us to finally turn to Him. Regardless of how long it takes, how old we are, how sinful we've been, or deeply we've grieved Him, *He is there* and longs for us to call on Him.

Because He is sovereign and gave us free will, He cannot come to our rescue until we invite Him into our hearts. Until our last breath, He will forgive our sins and accept us into His kingdom. But *WHY* would we wait to receive a Savior, a life of joy and peace? *WHY* fight evil and the world on our own? *WHY* struggle and try to control what we can *never* control? It is futility and lack of humility that stops us. We must realize that we can have a life worth considering, and a lifestyle worth imitating, through Christ Jesus.

Today, if I don't know Christ, I will ask Him to come into my heart, forgive my sins, take my problems and worries, and replace them with prosperity, peace and joy. If I am a follower of Jesus Christ, I will reconfirm my faith and love and thank Him for my new life. I refuse to wait another minute or for the next tragedy to acknowledge my Lord and Savior, to turn over my burdens, and to start living a truly blessed life.

Romans 10: 9-10, NKJV

That if you confess with your mouth the Lord Jesus and believe in your heart that God has raised Him from the dead. You will be saved. For with the heart one believes unto righteousness and with the mouth confession is made unto salvation.

Revelations 22:17, NKJV

And the Spirit and the bride say, "Come!" And let him who thirsts come. Whoever desires, let him take the water of life freely.

Hebrews 7:25, NKJV

Therefore, He is also able to save to the uttermost those who come to God through Him, since He always lives to make intercession for them.

"Vanity...My Favorite Sin" (from the Movie, "The Devil's Advocate")

Vanity of vanities, says the Preacher; Vanity of vanities, all is vanity.

– Ecclesiastes 1:2, NKJV

According to Strong's Concordance, the word vain or vanity has the idea of vapor or breathe. The connotation is that it is fleeting, empty, worthless, or useless.[3]

Here is a clear definition of what pride is: An inordinate self-esteem; an unreasonable feeling of superiority as to one's talents, beauty, wealth, rank, and so forth; disdainful behavior or treatment; insolence or arrogance of demeanor; haughty bearing.

All sin comes from pride or vanity. When we put ourselves first, before all others and all things, we are going against God's Word and the Holy Spirit.

The first murder recorded in the Bible is when Cain killed his brother Abel. God favored Abel's gift over Cain's, causing him to be jealous. It was pride and vanity that caused Cain to sin against his brother.

Lucifer, the most beautiful and favored angel, was so prideful and vain, and he believed that he could be more powerful than God. His vanity and pride caused one third of the angels to fall from grace.

Vanity is pride, and pride will block God's provisions. When we become boastful, self-reliant and feel like we don't need God, he will break us, remove his blessings, and allow suffering in our lives.

We must always seek humility, humble ourselves before the Lord, and surrender our pride. God will break us of vanity by putting a person or situation before us that we can't overcome on our own. Like Jonah, who defied God's instructions and ended up in the belly of the whale. With no way out, Jonah humbled himself, calling out to God for help. Supernaturally, God opened the mouth of that whale and released him from the most impossible situation and certain death. The story of Jonah shows us that a situation that is impossible for man is always possible through God. We must recognize His power, surrender, and acknowledge He is sovereign, almighty God.

Christ, who was God and had everything, came to Earth with nothing. Raised by a carpenter, He had no wealth, education or social status, died amongst criminals, and was laid to rest in a borrowed tomb. He spread His message through the misfits, unwanted, poor and meek. Jesus, King of all Nations, lived a life of humility and service to His Heavenly Father.

As a follower of Jesus Christ, we cannot be boastful and proud, but must live as He did, having a spirit of servitude. Jesus tore down the mighty religious temple because of the prideful Pharisees, and in the same way vanity will tear down our lives. When we release our pride and vanity, He rebuilds us and takes control. In our weakness, He is strong.

Today, I surrender my vanity and pride. Without Jesus Christ as my Lord and Savior, I would be nothing. Father, I pray that you will make me humble before you, cleanse me of self-centered behavior, let me surrender my ego. I acknowledge all of my strength comes from you. Please give me a spirit of humility that I may honor you. Let me look through the eyes of Christ in everything I do.

Matthew 5:3-11, NKJV

Blessed are the poor in spirit, for theirs is the kingdom of heaven. Blessed are those who mourn, for they shall be comforted. Blessed are the meek, for they shall inherit the earth. Blessed are those who hunger and thirst for righteousness, for they shall be filled. Blessed are the merciful, for they shall obtain mercy. Blessed are the pure in heart, for they shall obtain mercy. Blessed are the pure in heart, for they shall see God. Blessed are the peacemakers, for they shall be called sons of God. Blessed are those who are persecuted for "righteousness sake," for theirs is the kingdom of heaven. Blessed are you when they revile and persecute you and say all kinds of evil against you falsely for my sake. *

*Referred to as **The Beatitudes.** The Beatitudes are eight blessings recounted by Jesus in the Sermon on the Mount in the gospel of Matthew. They portray that humility, those who are humble before God (His children) are who will receive His rewards, blessings and keys to Heaven. The phrase *"inherit the earth"* is also similar to "theirs is the Kingdom of Heaven." A refined meaning of this phrase has been seen to say that those who are quiet or nullified will one day inherit the world. *Meek* in the Greek literature of the period most often meant gentle or soft.

And I Will Find Solace in Jehovah, God!

The Lord is my shepherd; I shall not want. He makes me to lie down in green pastures; He leads me beside the still waters. He restores my soul; He leads me in the path of righteousness. For His name's sake. Yes, though I walk through the valley of the shadow of death, I will fear no evil; For You are with me; Your rod and Your staff, they comfort me. You prepare a table before me in the presence of my enemies; You anoint my head with oil; My cup runs over. Surely goodness and mercy shall follow me All the days of my life; And I will dwell in the house of the Lord Forever.

– Psalms 23 1-6, NKJV

One of the first scriptures we are taught as children is Psalms 23. It encapsulates the peace of God, how He protects and loves us, and shows that He will deliver us from our enemies. During times of turmoil, pandemics, physical ailments, or any attack from the enemy, He is our refuge. When we see no end in sight to our suffering, He is with us. The enemy can take our jobs, our loved ones, our money, our health (for he comes to steal and destroy), but he cannot take our peace unless we give it to him. Serenity is ours and eternal, as long as we trust in our Heavenly Father. "This too shall pass" is a promise from God, and only if we give up and give in, will we lose our peace.

God's constant message to us is "I've got you," and He does. The enemy can weaken us through his attacks and make us question, "Where are you Lord, have you left me and forsaken me?" It's when we are weak that the evil one can take hold and break our spirit, communion, and trust in our Heavenly Father. We must resist this temptation to believe what the enemy tells us: "God doesn't care about you, you are not worthy, or He has abandoned you." These are LIES! He will never leave us; this is God's promise. In weakness and confusion, we must never forget this.

Today, I give thanks to my Heavenly Father for His strength is mine! I will resist the temptation to give in to the enemy and believe his lies. I refuse to surrender to weakness, confusion, or fear, and I find solace that God is always with me. If going through hard times, I will shift my focus, face my enemies or circumstances with His strength, and rest in His promise that He is always with me.

Deuteronomy 31:6, NKJV

Be strong and of good courage, do not fear nor be afraid of them; for the Lord your God, He is the One who goes with you, and He will not leave you nor forsake you.

Hebrews 13:5, NKJV

Let your conduct be without covetousness; be content with such things as you have. For he Himself has said, "I will never leave you nor forsake you."

When Bad Is Good
and Good Is Bad...

*How horrible it will be for those who call evil good and
good evil, who turn darkness into light and light into darkness, who turn what is bitter into something sweet and what
is sweet into something bitter.*

—Isaiah 5:20, NKJV

We must be so careful not to fall into darkness and
be influenced by the media and the constant barrage of
bad news. When we become addicted to hearing doom
and gloom and lose sight of the goodness of God, it defiles our souls. The temptation to listen about others
who are suffering is great, because we think this makes
our lives look better, that it is somehow a measurement
to our own success or happiness.

The advancement of technology and the reach of
broadcast can be used for good, but also for evil. It is so
important that we recognize the numbing effect that

constant exposure to bad and evil has on our minds and spirits. We become apathetic, negative, and depressed. There must be balance in this world, and the scales are tipping towards darkness, leaving us with feelings of total hopelessness and despair.

Since the first iPhone in 2002, there has been a decline in society and an increase in social distancing becoming our new reality—starting way before the 2020 pandemic. As Christians, we must govern ourselves and limit our exposure to all of the negative hype and hysteria. Put down the phones and iPads; turn off the televisions, radios, and computers. We must pick up the Bible, search for positive messages, and commune with other believers. When conversations turn to the latest bad news, gossip, condemnation, and hatred of others, we must walk away.

I am not saying that we can never be exposed to the media or technology, only that we must limit our exposure and balance our minds, bodies, and souls. Remembering, at all times, that God is in control, nothing happens that He doesn't allow to happen, and, in times that seem hopeless, He is our hope. Remember His promise that goodness and mercy will be with us all the days of our lives.

Today, I will turn off the television, the computer, the telephone. I will *unplug* and spend time with my family and friends. I will find positive messages in the book of Psalms, and rest in the knowledge that my Father in Heaven will always uphold me in His righteous right hand. I will not engage in gossip or focus on negative thoughts. I will find and share an encouraging message and turn over to God all of my fears and anxieties. I will seek (His) good, turn away from bad, and rebuke the enemy's message that bad is good and good is bad.

Psalms 25:3-5, NKJV

Indeed, let no one who waits on You be ashamed; Let those be ashamed who deal treacherously without cause. Show me Your ways, O Lord; Teach me Your paths. Lead me in Your truth and teach me, for you are the God of my salvation; On You I wait all the day.

Psalms 119:1-2, NKJV

Blessed are the undefiled in the way, who walk in the law of the Lord! Blessed are those who keep His testimonies, who seek Him with the whole heart!

Psalms 23:6, NKJV

...goodness and mercy shall follow me all the days of my life.

"Runnin' on Empty!"

I am the LORD your God, who brought you up out of the land of Egypt. Open your mouth wide, and I will fill it.
—Psalm 81:10, NKJV

Emptiness is a difficult emotion to describe. It may come from a loss of a relationship, job, loved one, or just an overwhelming lack of fulfillment in our lives. When we feel empty or weak, it's like a piece of our soul is missing. It can manifest into feelings of fatigue, depression, or even addiction. Often times, we seek anything that will fill our emptiness including drugs or alcohol.

If we become tempted to "self-medicate" in order to mask our feelings of emptiness, it will lead us down a very dark path. Turning to drugs or alcohol may feel good in the beginning but will ultimately compound our troubles and make us feel worse than we ever imagined. Addiction takes us away from God and those we love and will lead to isolation and the deepest sense of emptiness. We must rebuke the enemy when he whispers in our ears, "a drink or pill will make you feel better." We must avoid going down this road at all costs.

God's word holds the promise to combat our emptiness and will lead us to finding fulfillment in Christ. His Word is our fuel, nourishing our souls. It fills us with joy, contentment, and strength. Just as our bodies get weak if we don't eat, our spirits become fatigued if we don't feed it with God's Word.

Today, in my emptiness, I will fill this void with God's Word, selecting one or two versus to meditate and dwell on. I diligently seek the well-grounded assurance that when all earthly help and comfort fails, God himself will be the strength of my heart and my portion forever. I will not let the enemy steal my strength which I have through Christ Jesus. I will not surrender my peace and joy. I will remember that hopelessness and emptiness are just a state of mind and I will be filled with your promises and Living Word.

2 Corinthians 12:10, NKJV

For the sake of Christ, then, I am content with weaknesses, insults, hardships, persecutions, and calamities. For when I am weak, then I am strong.

Romans 15:13, NKJV

May the God of hope fill you with all joy and peace in believing, so that by the power of the Holy Spirit you may abound in hope.

Isaiah 40:31, NKJV

But those who wait on the Lord shall renew their strength; they shall mount up with wings like eagles, they shall run and not be weary, they shall walk and not faint.

Psalms 18:32, NKJV

It is God who arms me with strength and makes my way perfect.

Always Be Thankful

Be anxious for nothing, but in everything by prayer and supplication, with thanksgiving, let your request be made known to God; and the peace of God, which surpasses all understanding, will guard your hearts and minds through Christ Jesus.

—Philippians 4:6-7, NKJV

It is so easy to get in the pattern of asking for our desires and disregard God's will for us. Like a small child who only knows of his own needs, we become laser focused on asking our Father for everything we feel is lacking. We are children of God, and He loves to bless us, show us favor, and give us more than we deserve. When He withholds or takes something away, it is because He has a plan for us. We must learn to be grateful for what we have, and always be thankful.

God has planned our lives from who our parents are to who we marry, the children we may or may not have, and even our career paths. If we think about the complexity of our DNA and how each one of us are completely unique, then we must acknowledge His sovereignty. Our names have already been written in His book of life, and that alone should bring us complete satisfaction and thankfulness.

There have been times in my life that I've worried about the most basic things—shelter and food—and found myself begging the Father day after day for relief. To pray with fear in your heart is to pray without faith. Only when we pray, thankful in all things (good and bad), do we align ourselves with the Holy Spirit and get in the will of God. Once we surrender and really understand that He is in control, we can find serenity. I also look back on times when there seemed no way out of my situation, and I recognize He was always there. I was never alone, and all of my needs were met. I have never been homeless, hungry, or without clothing, and everything in my life has always worked out for the good. (see Romans 8:28 NKJV)

Finally, we should understand that God has a plan for us and learn to pray with discernment. When we recognize that He already sees our needs then there is no reason to ask for those things but give thanks. This allows us to speak to our Heavenly Father without fear or anxiety. We no longer waste our precious time with Him, going over a "wish list," but instead spend it strengthening our relationship, asking for His will to be done.

Today, I will remember that our Father already knows what I need, and I will avoid the temptation of asking for all of the things I don't have. I will acknowledge that He is sovereign and will rest in the fact that He supplies all of my needs. I ask my Heavenly Father that His will be done and focus on an intimate relationship with Him. I will thank Him for meeting all of my needs and the blessings in my life.

Job 34:19, NKJV

Yet He is not partial to prices, nor does He regard the rich more than the poor; for they are all the work of His hands.

1 Timothy 6:7-8, NKJV

For we brought nothing into this world, and it is certain we can carry nothing out. And having food and clothing, with these we shall be content.

God's Love Revealed

For God so loved the world, that he gave his only begotten son, that who so ever believes in him, shall not perish but have everlasting life.

—John 3:16, NKJV

The death and resurrection of Jesus gave His believers victory over the world and defeated fearfulness, faithlessness, and fruitlessness. For on the cross, He bore our sins, took the sting out of death, and gave all who believe in Him everlasting life!

He gave us the gift of righteousness. On the cross, Jesus became sin, received our sin, and all of the judgement and curse of sin fell on Him. Now all of the blessings, through His sacrifice, are ours! It has nothing to do with how good we are, but how good *He* is.

And on the third day, He gathered all the saints, released them into Heaven, and was resurrected. He rose from death so that we, through Him, have conquered death and received life everlasting.

Jesus did not have to come die a treacherous death on the cross; He chose to come and chose the sacrifice because He *LOVES* us! There was no greater sacrifice from our Heavenly Father than to turn His back on His only Son to let *Him* suffer, forsaking *Him* to bear the sins of the world.

And we now can celebrate for *He* has Risen!

Today, I celebrate the death and resurrection of my Lord and Savior, Christ Jesus! I will give thanks to God for His greatest sacrifice, His Son, and receive His mercy and grace. I rejoice in the Good News that, by *Him* and through *Him*, I receive forgiveness, peace, joy, and eternal life, and I will spread this good news to all!

John 17:22-23, NKJV

And the glory which You gave Me I have given them, that they may be one just as We are one; I in them, and You in Me; that they may be made perfect in one, and that the world may know that You have sent Me, and have loved them as You have loved Me.

John 10:10, NKJV

"I have come so that you can have life and have it more abundantly."

Luke 23:24, NKJV

And he said, "Father forgive them, for they know not what they are doing."

- A special note: Easter in the year 2020, during the time of the great pandemic/epidemic, churches were closed as social distancing was being imposed throughout the world. Through Christian broadcasts, there were a greater number of worshippers than has been seen in decades and possibly centuries!

Amazing Grace!!!

And he said to me, "My grace is sufficient for you, for My strength is made perfect in weakness."
—2 Corinthians 12:9, NKJV

John Newton was a slave trader in the 1700s. While serving on a slave ship, he did not get along with the crew, so they deserted him. Newton was left with a slave trader, who gave him to an African Princess, where he was enslaved and treated vilely. Finally, his father sent one of his sea captains to rescue John. On the voyage home they encountered a horrendous storm, and the ship started to sink. It was then that John cried out to God; miraculously, the ship's cargo shifted, covering a hole in the hull, and the vessel drifted to safety. Newton took this as a sign from the Almighty God and marked it as his conversion to Christianity. He started reading the Bible and became more sympathetic to his captives. However, he would later write, "I cannot consider myself to have been a believer in the full sense of the word, until a considerable time afterwards."[4]

God's grace falls quickly on some and more slowly on others. It is not as some may believe that it comes like a lightning bolt where everything in our life suddenly changes, and all worries and sorrows are lost. There seems to be an alignment that must take place between our mind and soul. It's almost like an internal battle to reconcile what is reasonable and what is amazing.

Our Father lays out different paths for each of us, with the ultimate goal that we fully surrender to Him and accept that He is Almighty, full of grace and love for us. Whether it comes in an instant or takes a lifetime, we must constantly strive for this perfection. When we live under the power of the Holy Spirit, we will continue to move towards a sanctified life. Once we receive God's grace, our lives are changed forever, and His goodness and mercy will follow us for the rest of our days!

Today, I surrender my mind and soul to Christ Jesus and ask for my Heavenly Father's Amazing Grace. If I am struggling, please help me seek your face, open my eyes, and let me see and accept the blessings of a fully sanctified life. I thank you, *for once I was lost, but now I'm found, was blind, but now I see!*" (John Newton, "Amazing Grace")

1 Corinthians 2:5, NKJV

That your faith should not be in the wisdom of men but in the power of God.

Isaiah 42:6, NKJV

...I will keep You and give You as a covenant to the people, As a light to the Gentiles, to open blind eyes...

*John Newton wrote "Amazing Grace" in 1772. It is performed over ten million times a year and has appeared in over eleven thousand albums. Recorded by such greats as Elvis, Aretha Franklin, Willie Nelson, and Johnny Cash, it has also been made into a Broadway musical.

Mission Impossible

For you will not leave my soul in Sheol.

—Psalms 16:10 NKJV

"Sheol (/ˈʃiːoʊl/ SHEE-ohl, /-əl/; Hebrew שְׁאוֹל Šə'ōl), in the Hebrew Bible, is a place of darkness to which spirits of the dead go. Under some circumstances, they are thought to be able to be contacted by the living. Sheol is also called Hades."[5]

Immediately following the crucifixion, the earth became dark; it shook and trembled, and there were great storms. As the followers of Jesus mourned the loss and fell into hopelessness, they prepared His body for burial. Although they had been told by Jesus that He would return, it wasn't something they truly believed, because they had no understanding. As the following day was the Sabbath, they waited for the first day of the week to visit the tomb where He was laid. Now on the first day, Mary Magdalene went to the tomb early while it was still dark and saw that the stone had been taken away from the tomb. (See John 20:1, NKJV)

Confusion broke loose amongst the disciples, as they believed the body of Jesus had been stolen. Only when Jesus appeared to Mary did they start to understand that He had risen (See John 20:15 NKJV).

For the two days prior to Him appearing to Mary Magdalene, the disciples hope had been lost, the mission of Christ abandoned. They certainly had to feel that what once seemed possible was now impossible and hope of continuing His mission became dashed. The disciples, through fear and weakness, abandoned everything Jesus had taught and prepared them for. They hid, waiting for certain death.

But Jesus knew that what was impossible for man would be possible through His power. So, when He departed from Earth, He empowered them (to carry out His mission) by sending the Holy Spirit. Once the disciples received this power, the mission became clear.

And what started with One (Man) and His twelve disciples began the movement (Mission Impossible) that changed the world forever. There are now an estimated 2.3 billion Christians in the world today.

Today, I accept the power within me to continue Jesus's mission through the Holy Spirit that dwells within me. As a follower of Jesus Christ, I recognize that all things are possible through Him, who died on the cross for me. I will join His mission to spread the Gospel through the power of the Holy Spirit and rejoice in the knowledge that He resides in me forever and ever!

Psalms 18:7, NKJV

Then the earth shook and trembled;

John 20:9, NKJV

For as yet they did not know the Scripture, that He must rise again from the dead.

Acts 2:2, NKJV

And suddenly there came a sound from heaven, as of a rushing mighty wind, and it filled the whole house where they were sitting...and they were all filled with the Holy Spirit...

Acts 1:8, NKJV

But you shall receive power when the Holy Spirit has come upon you; and you shall be witnesses to Me in Jerusalem, and in all Judea and Samaria, and to the end of the earth.

Mission Accomplished!!!

After this, Jesus, knowing that all things were now accom-
plished, that the Scripture might be fulfilled, said, "I thirst!"
Now a vessel full of sour wine was sitting there; and they filled
a sponge with sour wine, put it on hyssop, and put it to His
mouth. So, when Jesus had received the sour wine, He said,
"It is finished!" And bowing His head, He gave up His spirit.
                                        —John 19:28-30, NKJV

The resurrection of Jesus is the most critical part of
Christianity and the total foundation of the believer's
life. If not for Jesus rising from the dead, sin would not
have been defeated, and we would face certain death.
If not for the resurrection, Jesus would be considered
a prophet, a good and morale man, but not *The Christ*.

Jesus came with a mission to tell the truth, as well as
teach us how to live and pray. He gave us the gift of the
Holy Spirit and *hope*. His message included showing

us how to live an abundant, successful life full of peace and joy. Christ came to give us the assurance of eternal life. That anyone who believes in Him will one day be with our Father in Heaven.

In just three years, Jesus trained twelve men to spread "The Gospel." Yet this short mission, through His death and resurrection, was accomplished, and the movement (of spreading His Word) continues two thousand years later.

We now have HOPE, instead of hopelessness. We are restored, yesterday, today, and tomorrow. Regardless of our transgressions, He has paved the way and prepared a place for us in Heaven. He has granted us salvation and eternal life.

Today, I celebrate the resurrection of my Lord and Savior, Christ Jesus, and His "mission accomplished." I believe with all of my heart and soul that Christ is alive, has risen from the dead, and sits at the right hand of the Father. I proclaim my love for Jesus and look forward to the day when we meet face to face! My faith and hope are restored, my trust in Him unfaltering, I claim to the world that I am HIS, and my eternal soul belongs to *HIM. HE* lives within me. I wait, anxiously, for the day when my body dismisses my spirit, and I will dwell in Heaven forever and ever. Blessed is HE who has risen!

John 11:25-26, NKJV

"I am the resurrection and the life. He who believes in Me, though he may die, he shall live. And whoever lives and believes in Me shall never die."

John 14: 6, NKJV

"I am the way, the truth and the life, No one comes to the Father except through Me."

Acts 4, NKJV

"Nor is there salvation in any other, for there is no other name under heaven given among men by which we must be saved."

He Who Learns to Walk Away, Lives to Fight Another Day!

For we do not wrestle against flesh and blood, but against principalities, against powers, against the rulers of the darkness of this age, against spiritual hosts of wickedness in the heavenly places.

—Ephesians 6:12, NKJV

When we are filled with the Holy Spirit, He gives us boldness and courage, as well as a desire to fight for what is good and right. However, being a "right fighter" is futile. We might win the present battle, but we certainly won't win the war. When our desire to be right outweighs our desire to be obedient, we allow Satan to take hold, giving him power over us. As followers of Jesus Christ, we must focus on *His* mission, rely on *His* strength, and put on *His* armor before marching into war.

While Jesus was in the desert for forty days and His (human) body weak, Satan attacked, knowing if Christ went to the cross, the war was over. Jesus, knowing the enemy and recognizing his physical weakness, did not try and fight in His own strength but used the strength of the Father and the Word against the enemy. Certainly, Jesus, as God, could've won that battle, and yet He knew that the war was in Golgotha on the cross. And through God's Word, He resisted the devil, causing him to flee. Jesus chose to fight another day.

The enemy does not bother with non-believers. He is looking to win the souls of believers, and we must always be prepared to face the trials and tribulations he will put before us. In our own strength, his powers will defeat us every time. If we try and engage with him, we will not only lose the battles, but lose the war. We can only face him through the strength of Christ, His love, and His power. Our battle with evil will last until the end of time, and only when we armor ourselves with the power of the Word and the promise of God, do we learn to walk away and live to fight another day!

Today, I will pick my battles, and walk away, recognizing that my strength and power is in Christ Jesus. I know that trying to fight against the spiritual hosts of wickedness is a battle that cannot be won on my own.

I will retreat in my weakness, put on the armor of God, and wait to fight in *His* time and with *His* strength!

Ephesians 6:10-11, NKJV

Finally, my brethren, be strong in the Lord and in the power of His might. Put on the whole armor of God, that you may be able to stand against the wiles of the devil.

Ephesians 6: 13, NKJV

Therefore, take up the whole armor of God, that you may be able to withstand in the evil day, and having done all, to stand.

You Must Be ALL IN!!!

This is the work of God, that you believe in Him whom He sent.

—John 6: 29, NKJV

Sticking your toe in the water doesn't make you a swimmer, just as saying something needs salt won't make you a food critic! In life, we may be a "jack of all trades" but in faith there is only ONE way. That is *ALL THE WAY, ALL IN!!!*

For something so simple and easy to comprehend, it is mind boggling how many of us struggle to fully surrender. A true believer accepts that Jesus is the way to salvation and eternal life, and Scripture makes it crystal clear there is no other way.

Yes, Jesus is the only way to heaven; Jesus Himself says in the book of John, "I am the way, the truth, and the life. No one comes to the Father except through me"

(John 14:6, NKJV). He is not a way, as in one of many; He is the only way.

Unfortunately, about 40% of those who claim to be Christians believe there are other ways to receive salvation, but that is not biblical. The New Testament tells us that Jesus holds the key to our eternity, and only those who believe will enter the kingdom of God. Only when we finally grasp that Christ is the only way to salvation will our names be written in the Lamb's Book of Life. He holds the only key to Heaven.

Those who claim, "as long as someone is a good person, they will go to heaven," are dead wrong. This is false doctrine, and if they do not receive Jesus as their Lord and Savior (before death), they will be condemned on judgement day. That is why sharing the Gospel is the most important thing we will ever do. The message is simple. Jesus Christ is the one and only way to salvation and eternal life.

Today, if I have never received Christ as my Lord and Savior, I will find a believer to pray for me and lead me in the Sinner's prayer. If I am a follower of Jesus Christ, I will take inventory and recommit to Him that *I AM ALL IN!* I recognize that even though He waits for me, He will never force me to commit myself fully to Him. I claim for all to hear Jesus, You are my Lord and Savior, please forgive me of my sins. I completely surrender myself to You and believe that no one will see the gates of Heaven except through You. I ask that you receive me now, in my brokenness, and thank you for the blood that you shed for me on the cross.

John 10:25-30, NKJV

I told you, and you do not believe. The works that I do in My Father's name, they bear witness of Me. But you do not believe, because you are not of My sheep, as I said to you. My sheep hear My voice and I know them, and they follow Me. And I give them eternal life, and they shall never perish; neither shall anyone snatch them out of My hand. My Father, who has given them to Me, is greater than all; and no one is able to snatch them out of My Father's hand. I and My Father are one.

Psalms 23:6, NKJV

Surely goodness and mercy shall follow me All the days of my life; And I will dwell in the house of the Lord Forever.

Finding a "New Normal"

There's promise and beauty in so many things if we are open to it. Even through the darkest moments, if we try and see the light, there is promise in this as well.

– Natalie Bacho

When we face a tragedy like the loss of a loved one, a job, marriage or health, it changes our lives forever. Enduring a great loss alters who we are. Everything we once knew as normal is gone, and we are left struggling to figure out how to move forward. Whatever the loss may be, it is natural to find ourselves frozen in time, and yearning for our life to go back as it was before the tragedy.

It is so easy to withdraw, shut down, and ignore that the world still goes on with or without us. Giving up can sound so much easier than facing our new reality. If we continue mourning what has been lost and focus on what we once had, then we can fall into deep depression and overwhelming feelings of helplessness. This is when we must lean on our Heavenly Father, trust in Him, and ask Him to deliver us from our old life into the new life He has prepared for us.

Even though the disciples had been forewarned by Jesus of His death, they were not prepared when it actually happened. They were devastated by such a great loss and couldn't imagine life without Him. Afraid to meet as a group, each one of them would have felt isolated and overwhelmed about the future. The disciples would have felt anxious, depressed, and hopeless.

However, Jesus, knowing all things, came back for a short time to comfort them and reassure them of His promises. Jesus sent the Holy Spirit to inspire them to keep going and begin the process of healing. Although they could no longer see Jesus, He never left them, nor will He leave us. Eventually, they began new lives, fulfilling their new purpose of spreading the gospel and building the church, the body of Christ.

We are never alone through tragedy, and God is always with us as we navigate change in our lives. Although we can never get back what has been lost, we can learn to live a new normal and fulfill our new purpose in life. When we pray for comfort, the Holy Spirit will fill our bodies, minds, and souls, and we will feel the presence of Jesus. Just as the disciples, He will give us the strength and courage to move forward.

Today, I am facing a tragic loss. Father, I am overwhelmed with sorrow and can't imagine what my future holds. I ask you, in the name of Jesus Christ, to fill me with the Holy Spirit and let me feel His loving presence. It is through you I will find the strength and the courage to move forward and not dwell on the past. Please Father, help me find a new normal and continue my journey with you until the day I will join you and my loved ones in Heaven. There will be a new dawn and a new day!

Revelations 21:4, NKJV

And God will wipe away every tear from their eyes; there shall be no more death, nor sorrow, nor crying. There shall be no more pain, for the former things have passed away.

And It WAS Finished!!!!

And about the ninth hour Jesus cried out with a loud voice saying, "My God My God, why have You forsaken me?" Some of those who stood there, when they heard that, said, "This Man is calling for Elijah!" Immediately one of them ran and took a sponge, filled it with sour wine and put it on a reed, and offered it to Him to drink. The rest said, "let Him alone; let us see if Elijah will come to save Him. And Jesus cried out again with a loud voice and yielded up His spirit. Then behold, the veil of the temple was torn in two from top to bottom; and the earth quaked, and the rocks were split, and the graves were opened; and many bodies of the saints who had fallen asleep were raised; and coming out of the graves after His resurrection, they went into the holy city and appeared to many. So, when the centurion and those with him, who were guarding Jesus saw the earthquake and the things that had happened, they feared greatly saying, "truly this was the Son of God!"
—Matthew 27: 46-54, NKJV

Many Theologians believe that the sour wine represents all the sins of the world, and once received, Jesus released His spirit. This transfer had to be completed that we may all receive total forgiveness and full atonement. This finalized the ultimate transaction, defeating the enemy as Jesus washed away the sins of the world. Through the blood of the cross, we received forgiveness of sin and God's promise to never leave nor forsake us. It also gave us the assurance that when we leave our bodies here on Earth, we will immediately be in paradise, where Jesus will be waiting for us at the Father's right hand.

This is a very short and simple message, but so powerful as it is the foundation of Christianity. We know that all of our sins, past, present, future are forgiven. For centuries, people have tried to convolute the meaning of this sacrifice and what it did for us. Many religions teach that we must continually atone for our sins, but that is not biblical or true. When Jesus gave up His Spirit on the Cross "It was finished!" The minute we receive salvation, our sins are washed away, and we are new in Christ.

Today, I thank you, Jesus, for taking my sins and bearing them on the cross. I take comfort that all of the promises are fulfilled, and I receive total forgiveness and atonement through the "Final Transaction" on the cross. I know that immediately, when I am absent from the body, I will be present with the Lord. And even though I am not worthy, I receive Your redemption through *His* blood. I declare, "It is finished!" Because of Your sacrifice, I can truly walk as one with my Lord and Savior, Christ Jesus!

John 19: 28-30, NKJV

After this, Jesus knowing that all things were now accomplished, that the Scripture might be fulfilled, said, "I thirst!" Now a vessel full of sour wine was sitting there; and they filled a sponge with sour wine, put it on hyssop, and put it to His mouth. So, when Jesus had received the sour wine, He said, "It is finished!" And bowing His head, He gave up His spirit.

Psalms 69:21, NKJV

They also gave me gall for my food, and for my thirst they gave me vinegar to drink.

It's Okay to Talk to God

And when you pray, you must not be like the hypocrites. For they love to stand and pray in the synagogues and at the street corners, that they may be seen by others. Truly, I say to you, they have received their reward. But when you pray, go into your room and shut the door and pray to your Father who is in secret. And your Father who sees in secret will reward you. And when you pray, do not heap up empty phrases as the Gentiles do, for they think that they will be heard for their many words. Do not be like them, for your Father knows what you need before you ask him.

—Matthew 6: 5-10, NKJV

For most of us there has been a religious doctrine that has influenced the way that we pray. Raised as a Presbyterian, my approach to prayer was very formal. For many years, I have prayed using a certain format at specific times and positions. Only after studying

Scripture for many years did it dawn on me that my prayers had been ineffective. God does not want "recited prayers" and certainly not "repetitive prayers," but He is looking for us to open our hearts and commune (talk) with Him.

Jesus tells us do not use vain repetition for that is what the heathen does (Matthew 6:7, NKJV). When we pray to our Heavenly Father, He is not counting the number of words we use or the length of our prayers. He seeks to know our hearts.

Although God knows all, sees the beginning and the end, and already comprehends our thoughts and needs, it is important to communicate them through prayer. Speaking breathes life into our words.

Our Father in Heaven longs to have a personal relationship with each of His children, desires our dependence on Him, and wants us to build an unbreakable bond through constant dialogue. We do not have to be on our knees, heads bowed, and eyes closed to talk to our Heavenly Father. No matter where we are or what we are doing, it's okay to talk to God!

Like anything in life, when you first approach this new style of communication, it may seem uncomfortable and even hard. We can speak to our Heavenly Father just as we would our earthly father, sharing our burdens and fears. Once we realize God is there all of the time, waiting to hear from us, it becomes second nature talking to Him throughout the day. When this happens, we become unburdened, nothing overwhelms us, and we are filled with joy and peace.

Today, I will start talking to my Heavenly Father and staying in constant communication with Him throughout each and every day. I will not lean on my own understanding but His, allowing Him to guide and lead my decisions in life. I look forward to a life of peace and joy, knowing that He is with me, listening to me, and waiting for me to talk with Him.

Matthew 7: 7-11, NKJV

Ask, and it will be given to you; seek, and you will find; knock, and it will be opened to you. For everyone who asks receives, and the one who seeks finds, and to the one who knocks it will be opened. Or which one of you, if his son asks him for bread, will give him a stone? Or if he asks for a fish, will give him a serpent? If you then, who are evil, know how to give good gifts to your children, how much more will your Father who is in heaven give good things to those who ask him!

John 15:7, NKJV

If you abide in me, and my words abide in you, ask whatever you wish, and it will be done for you.

Don't Look Back, You Can Never Look Back!

Jesus said to him, "No one who puts his hand to the plow and looks back is fit for the kingdom of God."
—Luke 9:62, NKJV

If we drive our car looking in the rearview mirror, not only do we miss what is in front of us, but inevitably, we will crash and burn! The same is true for our lives. If we are always looking back, then we are filled with regrets and guilt. We must realize that there is nothing to gain from rewinding our lives or second guessing our decisions and paths. Once we realize that everything in the past is there for a reason (most often for our spiritual growth), then we can receive today's blessings and joy. What we can gain from our past is a new perspective and strengthened purpose.

When God destroyed Sodom and Gomorrah, He warned Lot and his family not to look back. However, Lot's wife succumbed to the temptation, and when she did look back, she turned to ashes. "But his wife, from behind him, looked back, and she became a pillar of salt" (Genesis 19:26, NKJV). In reality, I believe, in turning back, she got too close to the fire and burned with the cities.

Just as Jesus instructs us not to worry about the future, the same is true for the past; both are out of our control, and the sooner we learn this very important lesson, the sooner we will find peace and contentment in the present. We are made new in Christ, not only at the time we accept Him as our Savior, but every minute we can be renewed in Him.

We can't forget our past, for in it we find a way to change courses, straighten our paths, correct our mistakes, and make amends. However, if we choose to dwell in what's behind us, the present is wasted. If our Heavenly Father forgives all sins and transgressions, and we are born again through the blood of Jesus, then we must forgive ourselves, let go, and don't look back!

There is a reason for the distinction of our lives before and after Christ. The before, when we believed destiny was in our control, is washed away. We can rest in knowing that He has, and always will be, in control of our lives. Regardless of who we were or what transgressions we've made, the slate is wiped clean, and we are open to a brighter future. Looking back makes us depressed, looking ahead makes us stressed, but when looking above we will be blessed!

Today I pledge to stop dwelling on the past, wasting precious time, and losing focus on what is in front of me. If I have claimed salvation, then I will reclaim it. If I have never claimed salvation, I will find a follower of Jesus Christ to lead me through the sinner's prayer for deliverance. I count my blessings this moment, one moment at a time, and rest in the knowledge that my life has been laid out for me, long before I was born. I thank my loving Heavenly Father for forgiving all of my past transgressions and will enjoy the here and now. I embrace that the past is over, and it can touch me not!

Philippians 3: 13-15, NKJV

Brethren, I do not regard myself as having laid hold of it yet; but one thing I do, forgetting what lies behind and reaching forward to what lies ahead, I press on toward the goal for the prize of the upward call of God in Christ Jesus.

2 Corinthians 5:17, NKJV

Therefore, if anyone is in Christ, he is a new creation. The old has passed away; behold, the new has come.

S-P-A-R-E Me From Insanity!!!

God grant me the courage not to give up what I think is right even though I think it is hopeless.

—Chester W. Nimitz

The Lord takes pleasure in those who fear Him, in those who hope in His mercy.

—Psalms 147:11, NKJV

S – Spiritual – We can never lose sight of who we are in Christ. When we have nowhere to go, nothing to do, and life has got us down, He is always waiting for us to speak with Him, read His Word, and share our faith with others. Our spiritual connection with Him in times of adversity must remain strong.

P- Productive – An idol mind is the devil's workshop, and as human beings we need to feel self-worth. If we're not working, it doesn't mean we can't stay productive! Clean that closet. Volunteer. Master that recipe or art project. But be mindful in how you devote your time. Utilize and strengthen your body, mind, and spirit, and do everything for Christ!

A – Acceptance – We can accept our situation without accepting defeat. There may be nothing we can do to change our current circumstances; however, we can turn it over to Christ and let Him work the miracles, change the pace or place, and set us back on our paths.

R – Righteous – We are righteous in Christ. Circumstances happen, and we are not in control. How we handle our lives, especially adversity, *is* in our control! We should never be embarrassed, regardless of what's going on, and must always remain upright, excellent, and beyond reproach. We are the representatives of Christ here on earth, and people (especially non-believers) look to us, our behavior, and reactions, even more so when times are bad.

E – Exemplary – We must lead by example! We must show those we love and the world that no matter how bleak things may seem, we will remain Spiritual, Productive, Accepting, and Righteous!

When everything around us is falling apart and life seems to be on a downward spiral, it is easy to lose sight of good times. But if our lives were nothing but great all of the time, we would lose sight of our Lord's goodness. Regardless of our circumstances, whether it was our fault or out of our control, God makes a way, even when there seems to be no way. He will help us; there is no shame in trusting in Him, just ask because He already knows.

There is no time for pity, self-doubt, loss of faith or insanity. When we are down, God put us there, and it is up to each of us to see the reason why. If we let ourselves play the victim card, we immediately engage in a game with the devil, who wants us to lose all hope. He wants to destroy, but he will not prevail because God's love never fails. God will never forsake His children.

God can't lie; He is truth, and He will not leave us. If God allows us to be in a situation, rest assured that we have a brighter future on the other side. God's will may not be the easiest road, but it's the right road, and if it is His plan, we will not only get through it but be victorious and better than before.

Today I may be looking at unemployment, sickness, death, divorce, betrayal, or addiction—whatever adversity is facing me, *I am not alone!* I hold on to my relationship with Jesus and accept this is only temporary. I will remain righteous and exemplary. I thank my Heavenly Father for His deliverance and look forward to what He has in store for me. I ask in the name of Jesus, please spare me from insanity!

Deuteronomy 3:8, NKJV

"The LORD is the one who goes ahead of you; He will be with you. He will not fail you or forsake you. Do not fear or be dismayed."

Psalms 39:7, NKJV

And so, Lord, where do I put my hope? My only hope is in you.

Proverbs 23:18, NKJV

Surely there is a future, And your hope will not be cut off.

You Are NEVER Alone!

Who shall separate us from the love of Christ? Shall tribulation, or distress, or persecution, or famine, or nakedness, or danger, or sword? As it is written, "For your sake we are being killed all the day long; we are regarded as sheep to be slaughtered." No, in all these things we are more than conquerors through him who loved us. For I am sure that neither death nor life, nor angels nor rulers, nor things present nor things to come, nor powers, nor height nor depth, nor anything else in all creation, will be able to separate us from the love of God in Christ Jesus our Lord.

—Romans 8:35-39, NKJV

God does not promise us a life without troubles. What He does promise is to never leave us alone once we accept Christ as our Lord and Savior. When we are facing adversity, it is easy to think He's not with us.

Adversity usually comes from the action of others, especially if we are dealing with non-believers. Their actions and words are unfiltered or without a moral compass (the Holy Spirit) to guide them. They can be impossible to deal with and have no problem saying or doing things that are hurtful.

A great example of this is when Potifer's wife accused Joseph of making sexual advances towards her. Even though it was her who tried numerous times to trap him into committing adultery, the blame fell squarely (and unjustly) on Joseph, who suffered the consequences and was imprisoned. But if this had not happened, Joseph would never have met the King's baker or ended up in his powerful position serving the King. God never left Joseph alone but was with him every step of the way. What could have been terrible for Joseph, God turned to good.

It is normal to think when we accept the Holy Spirit into our lives that everything will be "smooth sailing." The truth is, most of what happens to us in life, is out of our control. What is in our control are the responses or actions we take. It is difficult when we feel attacked or threatened not to respond back with aggression towards our attacker. We take the bait and find ourselves engaging in a manner that doesn't match with our spirit or belief system.

We should avoid at all costs engaging in an argument or battle with others. Although it is hard, we must hold on to the fact that God is with us and will defend us, and we have no need to lower ourselves into this temptation. We need to agree to disagree, walk away from conflict, and show love where there is hate.

Trying to reason with or defend ourselves against a non-believer is futile and only leads to frustration. Sometimes we may have to walk away from those closest to us, including our families. Regardless, when we feel under attack or find ourselves about to engage in an argument, we must remember He is with us, we are not alone, and the battle is not ours.

Today, I face attacks from others and am tempted to fight and defend myself. I call on the Lord who is always with me to deal with this turmoil. I refuse to argue. I choose to walk away from conflict and will let my Heavenly Father deal with my enemies. I will walk in the light, shine my light on the darkness whenever possible, and remember I am never alone!

Josphua 1:5

"...I will be with you. I will not leave you nor forsake you."

John 14:16, NKJV

And I will ask the Father, and he will give you another Helper, to be with you forever.

When in Doubt... Wait!

For God has not given us a spirit of fear, but of power and of love and of a sound mind.

— 2 Timothy 1:7, NKJV

Doubt usually comes from fear of the unknown. Fear is what the enemy preys on, and it opens our minds and spirits to his lies. We must be so careful not to let Satan get inside our heads.

When our Lord speaks to us, His messages are clear and concise. When He gives us an answer, our spirit will be at peace, without doubt. Messages or thoughts that come from any other source, especially from the enemy, leave us with feelings of unrest and fearing what the outcome will be. Our Father will never lead us down the wrong path or astray from His living Word. So, when we are overcome with doubt or fear, it is time to sit back and wait, praying for God to agree or reject what is on our mind.

A good way to confirm our thoughts are from God is when we feel positive energy and an overwhelming sense of certainty. Thoughts that we have from anywhere else will release a negative energy and fill us with anxiety, doubt, and fear.

When we are walking in the Holy Spirit, there is a supernatural wisdom inside of us which provides the discernment we need to recognize where our thoughts (doubts) come from. It becomes very clear when we are given a message from God because He leaves no question as to what we should do. When worry takes hold, we must turn to His word and pray for His will. This will resolve who or where the message is coming from.

As we grow into sainthood, confusion of who is speaking to us will dissipate and make way to an understanding of when we should act and when we should wait. This comes through obedience and abiding in the living Word of God. We should also remember the outcomes and results of our previous actions and responses when we didn't turn our doubt over to God. When we react to thoughts and messages that are not from Him, we go down the wrong path, but it is never too late to seek His will. When we lose our way, all we need to do is call on our Father and He will get us back on point.

Our job is to be patient, wait for His answer, and not act on our own timeline, but His.

Today, let me see that the more I pray and meditate on His word, the easier it becomes for me to recognize the path I am to take. Through discipline, I will make less and less mistakes and ultimately walk in perfect harmony with Jesus Christ. The results are amazing; as I live in servitude towards Him, my life will be filled with blessing after blessing and accompanied by peace, joy, harmony, and love. As I become in tune with God's messages, I walk safely, without doubt, down my path.

Proverbs 20:25, NKJV

The fear of man brings a snare, but whoever trusts in the Lord shall be safe.

Mark 11:23, NKJV

For assuredly, I say to you, whoever says to this mountain, "Be removed and be cast into the sea," And does not doubt in his heart but believes that those things he says will be done, he will have whatever he says.

James 1:5-8, NKJV

If any of you lacks wisdom, let him ask God, who gives generously to all without reproach, and it will be given him. But let him ask in faith, with no doubting, for the one who doubts is like a wave of the sea that is driven and tossed by the wind.

For that person must not suppose that he will receive anything from the Lord; he is a double-minded man, unstable in all his ways.

Dealing with Betrayal

Then Peter came to Him and said, "Lord, how often shall my brother sin against me, and I forgive him: Up to seven times?" Jesus said to him, "I do not say to you, up to seven times, but up to seventy times seven.

—Matthew 18: 21-22, NKJV

Seventy signifies spiritual perfection. So "seventy times seven" means we need to forgive someone completely, and not let anger fester. Regardless of how many times a person betrays us, we must let it go and give to God each and every time.

The shear meaning of betrayal is a negative action taken against another; to lead astray or seduce; to fail or desert, especially in a time of need; to deliver to an enemy by treachery. Different from sin, which is self-afflicting, betrayal is intentional, harmful, and painful to others.

Our first look at betrayal in Scripture is against God, when Adam and Eve ate of the forbidden fruit. So, it has been with Man since the beginning of time. God had provided everything to Adam and Eve, asking only one thing—that they not eat from the tree of life. God's reaction to their disobedience was banishment from the Garden of Eden, taking away their privileged life.

The theme of betrayal continues all the way through the Bible. Cain and Abel, Sampson and Delilah, Joseph and his brothers, David and Bathsheba, and the ultimate betrayal of Judas Iscariot against Jesus. This recurring theme shows that betrayal is much like sin and at the core of mankind.

The worst kind of betrayal is when it comes from someone close to us, such as when a family member or loved one intentionally takes action to harm us. Often this will come at a time when we need them the most. This kind of betrayal is the hardest to forgive, but if we are true followers of Jesus Christ, we must find forgiveness in our hearts.

If someone betrays us, then we must ask, "Why does my brother or sister want to cause me harm? What is hurting in them? What would motivate them to betray me? What is their pain, sorrow, or grief? How can I help them?" As hard as this is in reality, if we don't try and reconcile with whoever has harmed us, it will only cause us more pain and heartache. This is why Jesus tells us we must forgive one another; not just one time but every time.

Today, I forgive everyone who has ever betrayed me, just as my Heavenly Father has forgiven me. I will go to my brother or sister and ask for forgiveness as I forgive them. I release any bitterness, anger, or resentment, and I ask my Heavenly Father to replace these negative feelings with love. I will pray for all who have ever come against me and find empathy for those who have hurt me the most.

Matthew 6: 14-15, NKJV

"For if you forgive men their trespasses, your heavenly Father will also forgive you. But if you do not forgive me their trespasses, neither will your Father forgive your trespasses.

Psalms 41:9

Even my own familiar friend in whom I trusted, Who ate my bread, Has lifted up his heel against me.

The Law of Reciprocity—Give and It Will Be Given Unto You.

"And try me on this," Says the Lord of hosts, "If I will not open for you the windows of heaven And pour out for you such blessing That there will not be room enough to receive it."
—Malachi 3:10, NKJV

"**Reciprocity** – mutual dependence, action or influence; a mutual exchange for privileges; the quality or state of being reciprocal."[6]

"**Tithe** – a tenth part of something paid as a voluntary contribution or as a tax especially for the support of a religious establishment. 2: the obligation represented by individual tithes."[7]

Jesus uses the parable of the sower in the book of Mark, chapter four. It is one of many that are told by

Him framed around the *Power of Giving*. It is easy to be confused by this and ask, "Well if someone doesn't have enough, how can he give?" (see Mark 4:26 NKVJ)

Reciprocity doesn't always mean a financial exchange, nor are there limits set for how it works. Tithing is giving ten percent of *what you have* that sets reciprocity in motion.

When Jesus talks about the sower preparing the ground for planting the seed, He is referring to our hearts. We must prepare our hearts first and foremost. Once the "seed for giving" is planted, our desire to bless others grows. Once we develop a spirit for giving and put this principle into action, it starts the inertia or energy in for which great blessings will be given unto us. This is God's law of reciprocity.

This can sound a little bit like a slippery slope. If in our hearts, we are only giving to receive, intentions are not right. The Lord loves a joyous giver, and this joy comes from the heart. It is something we cannot know until we start, but one thing is for sure: God challenges us to just try. Like everything else in our life, we can never out do Him.

There are five reasons that we do not give to the Lord:

Confusion - We don't know what the Word says

Consequence - We do not understand what we are missing

Confidence - We lack knowledge of the Lord's blessings when we tithe

Conviction - No one has ever taught us the important of giving

Carelessness - We overspend what we are given and therefore are "lacking" instead of "abundant"

Today, Father, I pray for the spirit of giving and for the understanding of being a good steward with my finances. Please speak to me and give me the conviction and confidence to give. Let me understand the law of reciprocity, that the more I give, the more will be given unto me. Remove my doubt and fear of letting go, and bless me, Heavenly Father, with Your favor.

Mark 4:26, NKJV

And He said, "For whoever has, to him more will be given; but whoever does not have, even what he has will be taken away from him."

Malachi 3:10 NKJV

Bring all the tithes into the storehouse, that there may be food in My house, And try Me now in this, Says the Lord of hosts, "If I will not open for you the windows of heaven And pour out for you such blessings that there will not be room enough to receive it."

The Existence of Evil

Let no one say when he is tempted, "I am tempted by God;"
for God cannot be tempted by evil, nor does He Himself tempt
anyone.

—James 1:13, NKJV

The book of Job is the oldest manuscript in the Bible. It validates that good and evil have always been in existence. It is something God wants us to be fully aware of. However, we don't have to worry, for our Heavenly Father and His infinite goodness will always prevail. We should have no fears. Evil has and will always abound (on Earth), but when we accept our salvation through the blood of Christ, the enemy can touch us not!

The story of Job is a about a wager between God and Satan. Satan challenged God that Job was only a true servant because he had all of the blessings on Earth, and if those were taken away, Job would no longer follow God. However, the Lord knew Job's heart and allowed Satan to take everything from Job—family, servants, friends, livestock, health, and wealth. It was an ultimate attack of evil!

Job was ridiculed and chastised by his closest friends and advisors who accused him of angering God. They lectured Job to admit his sin and repent, but the truth was he had not sinned. He had lost everything, including his health, and was covered with painful boils which caused insufferable pain. Through all this suffering and oppression from his closest friends, Job would not turn away from God. Finally, God removed Satan's power over Job and restored all that he had ten-fold. God knew and never doubted in His servant Job, and the devil fled, defeated once again!

Evil attacks are going to come to those who love the Lord. Therefore, we must equip ourselves for when Satan attacks. We should ask ourselves, "Am I living a life of sainthood and servitude like Job? Would I remain faithful, even grateful, if everything was taken from me?" When we completely surrender to our Father in Heaven and accept repentance through the cross, we gain His supernatural protection and power against the enemy. When we accept Jesus as our Lord and Savior, we are also accepting a life of servitude. Like Job, we must remain faithful, even grateful, regardless of trials or tribulations.

Today, I pray for protection from the enemy. Satan can tempt or even attack me, but he can't take my soul.

I belong to the Lord, and my strength is in Him. Father help me live a life of servitude, like Job, and remain faithful and grateful. Even if everything is taken from me, I can never lose Christ once I have claimed He is my Lord and Savior!

Job 1:21, NKJV

Naked I came from my mother's womb, and naked shall I return there. The Lord gave, and the Lord has taken away; Blessed be the name of the Lord.

Job 2:6-7, NKJV

And the Lord said to Satan, "Behold, he is in your hand, but spare his life." So, Satan went out from the presence of the Lord, and struck Job with painful boils from the sole of his foot to the crown of his head.

You Must Anchor Yourself in Jesus!

And we desire that each one of you show the same diligence, 'to the full assurance of hope, until the end, that you do not become sluggish, but imitate those who through faith and patience inherit the promise.

—Hebrews 6:11-12, NKJV

Longing or yearning versus faith and assurance can be likened to a house made of straw and a house made of stone. We all know the story of the three little pigs! The first two little pigs hoped their straw houses would stand against the wolf. The third little pig took his time building a house with stone and mortar, and therefore he had faith and assurance his house would stand. His house was so strong he was able to provide shelter to the other two. In real life, the wolf is Satan, who preys on our areas of weakness and then attacks. That is why we must build our lives on the cornerstone of Christ.

Another analogy is the anchor of a ship. If the ship is at sea when strong winds come without an anchor, she will be pushed in every direction. When a ship is anchored, it will stay in place and weather the storm.

Hope is when we try and lean on our own understanding. Faith is relying on God's Word, with the promise that His Son, Jesus Christ, came not only to give us salvation but strength in our own times of weakness. As we build our foundation in Him, our strength becomes unbreakable when the enemy attacks.

We must be anchored in Jesus to receive the promise of God. We can be hopeful things in our lives work out, but without a strong foundation, we can't be confident or assured that they will. Hope isn't enough when trials and tribulations come. That is when we find our house cannot withstand the storm; that our house is built of straw (hope) and not the cornerstone of Jesus Christ. Faith in Christ is our only assurance of protection against the evil one. He is our rock and unbreakable foundation.

Today, I pray to be anchored in Christ and have assurance that He will protect me against the enemy's attacks. Please, Father, help me build a solid foundation through Your Son, Jesus. He is the cornerstone of my house, and with Him, it will not fall. I will trust in the Lord with all my heart!

Isaiah 28:16, NKJV

So, this is what the Sovereign LORD says: "See, I lay a stone in Zion, a tested stone, a precious cornerstone for a sure foundation; the one who relies on it will never be stricken with panic.

Proverbs 3:5, NKJV

Trust in the Lord with all your heart, and lean not on your own understanding.

Isaiah 33:6, NKVJ

He will be the sure foundation for your times, a rich store of salvation and wisdom and knowledge; the fear of the LORD is the key to this treasure.

Persecution of Christians

Now brother will deliver up brother to death, and a father his child; and children will rise up against parents and cause them to be put to death. And you will be hated by all for My name's sake, but he who endures to the end will be saved.
—Matthew 10:21-23, NKJV

We are living in a time of genocide when Christians are persecuted and killed for their beliefs. The United States continues to remove God from schools, monuments, and public buildings. We can no longer pray publicly without the threat of being attacked. Christians are blinded by what is coming, as we allow this nation to lose its protection "under God." We are headed down a path of complete destruction.

The United States was founded by Christians who escaped from tyranny and unjust governments. Our Constitution was written by Christians. We are being stripped of our constitutional rights to speak and worship freely. We acquiesce to Sharia Law and other non-Christian principles that preach one message: destroy their enemies. Their ultimate goal is to overtake or kill those who do not follow the same beliefs.

At the beginning of the Chinese Revolution, the communist government burned Bibles and western books, destroyed churches, murdered ministers, and broke the legs of any citizen that refused to bow before Mao Tse-Tung. At that time, there were approximately 500,000 believers in their country. Today, there is an estimated 500 million believers in the Republic of China! This happened behind closed doors in secret, heart to heart and mouth to mouth.

This is a perfect example that faith can and will prevail. That each of us can make a difference. Nothing can stop the truth and spreading of the gospel of Jesus Christ! However, the time is now, and we must act before it's too late. Our great nation is in grave danger of losing our First Amendment Right to worship freely.

We can choose to make a difference and change the direction this world is heading. It starts by spreading the Gospel to all that we meet. We can engage those of different religions, cultures, and countries, as well as share the love of Jesus and let them know He died for their sins. Tell them the good news of eternal life. We can support financially and pray for those who spread

God's Word. We can support and vote for Christians. All believers need to join in constant corporate prayer. Each of us must stand in our faith, against persecution, without fear of the consequences.

Today, I mourn and pray for my brothers and sisters in Christ that are being persecuted and jailed for their beliefs. I pray for this nation and her leaders. I stand against the threat of death, without fear, proclaiming Jesus Christ is my Lord and Savior. I will join in corporate prayer against the dark principalities of this world. I choose to make a difference starting right now!

Matthew 10:28, NKJV

And do not fear those who kill the body. . .fear Him who is able to destroy both body and soul in hell.

2 Timothy 3:12, NKJV

Yes, and all who desire to live godly in Christ Jesus will suffer persecution.

Matthew 5:10, NKJV

Blessed are those who are persecuted for righteousness' sake, for theirs is the kingdom of heaven.

Prince of Peace

For unto us a Child is born. Unto us a Son is given; ....and His name will be called... Prince of Peace.

—Isaiah 9:6, NKJV

Each year, as we approach Christmas Day, we can't forget the true meaning for which we celebrate. Christmas by definition is Christians coming together for a feast in celebration of the day Jesus was born. When we busy ourselves in preparations for Christmas Day, it causes stress instead of joy.

It is easy to get caught up in the commercialization of Christmas and forget why we celebrate this most Holy Day. We should celebrate this day but not lose sight of the reason for the season: the miraculous birth of Jesus Christ, born of the virgin Mary. "Unto us a Child is born...and His name will be called Prince of Peace" (Isiah 9:6, NKJV). There is no greater gift or reason to celebrate than the birth of our Lord and Savior!

Today, I will focus on the most precious gift, the birth of Jesus Christ. Through the birth of God's perfect, sinless Son, I receive the Gift of Salvation and Eternal Life! This shall be my focus each year as Christmas day approaches. I will not get sidetracked and lose focus on the reason for the season. Through the immaculate conception of Mary's child, Jesus, and in fulfillment of the prophesy of Isaiah, I celebrate the birth of my Savior, the Prince of Peace. I give glory to my Father in Heaven and thanksgiving for the greatest gift on earth!

Matthew 1:23, NKJV

"Behold, the virgin shall be with child, and bear a Son, and they shall call His name Immanuel, which is translated, 'God with us."

Luke 2:11, NKJV

For there is born to you this day in the city of David a Savior, who is Christ the Lord.

Psalms 72:11, NKJV

Yes, all kings shall fall down before Him; all nations shall serve Him.

Mary, Mother of Jesus

And having come in, the angel said to her, "Rejoice, highly favored one, the Lord is with you; blessed are you among women!"

—Luke 1:28, NKJV

Consider Mary, mother of Jesus, who had known no man and was visited by the angel Gabriel, who told her she would conceive a child. She was a woman of devout faith and well-studied in scriptural teachings. No doubt, she would know of the prophesies concerning the birth unto a virgin of Immanuel, the Son of God.

Mary lived in a time of great darkness, under Roman law and persecution of the Jewish people. It was a time when many believers turned away from God. Mary was a devout young virgin, betrothed to a man named Joseph. When she was visited by Gabriel, she never questioned the angel's message or had doubt of such a miracle. Her only question was, "How can this be, since I do not know a man?" Once Gabriel explained that the birth would come through The Holy Spirit, she answered "Behold the maidservant of the Lord! Let it be to me according to your word" (Luke 1:38, NKJV)

Children can be a double-edged sword, as there is no deeper love or heartache for a parent. In Mary's life, there would be no greater elation or deeper sorrow, as the mother of Jesus. For her first son was born as a sacrifice for the world, and He was sealed for an unthinkable death. She knew her time with Him would be brief. She sat at the foot of the cross and witnessed Her firstborn son, suffering until death. There is no way to fully comprehend the depth of her sorrow. Yet she endured, through her obedience and faith in God.

When we think about Mary, mother of Jesus, she should inspire us to have her depth of faith. We should never rebuke or question the Lord's plan, but accept His will for our lives

Today, I pray for the faith and endurance of Mary, mother of Jesus. I see in comparison to Mary, my burdens have been light and my sorrows shallow. I give thanks to my Father in Heaven, for me, the gift of Jesus comes without struggle. For the only thing needed for salvation and eternal life is to accept Jesus Christ as my Lord and Savior.

Luke 1:26-27, NKJV

Now in the sixth month the angel Gabriel was sent by God to a city of Galilee named Nazareth, to a virgin betrothed to a man whose name was Joseph, of the house of David. The virgin's name was Mary.

Luke 1:34, NKJV

Then Mary said to the angel, "How can this be, since I do not know a man:"

Luke 1:38, NKJV

Then Mary said, "Behold the maidservant of the Lord! Let it be to me according to your word."

God's Words to Joseph

But while he thought about these things, behold an angel of the Lord appeared to him in a dream, saying, "Joseph, son of David, do not be afraid to take to you Mary your wife, for that which is conceived in her is of the Holy Spirit."

—Matthew 1:20, NKJV

During the time of Joseph, it was customary for people to marry and then wait a certain period of time before consummating their marriage. At the time of engagement, the vows had been taken, including the confirmation of the woman's virginity.

Can you imagine the struggle Joseph must have faced when Mary became pregnant? Knowing this, he could have easily dismissed Mary and accused her of breaking the marriage vows and disgracing his family name. He would have considered sending Mary away to something like a convent, never again to be seen in public. She could have faced a penalty of death, but certainly she would have been branded as an ungodly woman and faced accusations of harlotry, unworthy of marriage and banned from her community forever.

We will never know what Joseph was thinking when he found out that his betrothed was pregnant. Yet, he made the decision not to make her a public example and hid her until the child was born. This was before the angel appeared to him in a dream, giving Joseph confirmation of the "immaculate conception," and that His son, born from the House of David, was Christ the King.

Both Joseph and Mary faced an unbelievable challenge of ridicule, judgment, shame, humility, and persecution from the outside world. However, they followed God and endured the suffering.

They were most likely in their late teens when they were faced with this unfathomable situation. Their story should inspire all of us to have the level of faith of these young people.

Today, I ask "Am I able to put my faith in Christ Jesus beyond anything or anyone? If my faith is challenged and reputation in danger, will I sacrifice everything to follow the Lord?" I pray Father for the same level of faith and trust of Mary and Joseph. Give me the strength if faced with a hard decision to turn it over to you and not worry or seek approval from others. I will not question the challenges you set before me. I will seek humility and a heart of servitude and acknowledge your sovereignty.

Proverbs 3:5-6, NKJV

Trust in the Lord with all your heart and lean not on your own understanding; (but) in all your ways acknowledge Him, and He shall direct your paths.

Psalms 28:7, NKJV

The Lord is my strength and my shield; my heart trusted in Him, and I am helped; therefore, my heart greatly rejoices, and with my song I will praise Him.

Isaiah 26:4, NKJV

Trust in the Lord forever, for in Yah, the Lord, is everlasting strength.

My New Year Resolutions!

There is no want to those who fear him......But those who seek the Lord shall not lack any good thing.
—Psalms 34:9-10, NKJV

We proclaim our resolutions and promises at the beginning of each New Year. Lose weight, save money, pay off bills, get a new job, workout, and other things that will make us feel better about ourselves. Most of which serve our vanity and desires. How often do we keep these resolutions and promises? Are they not fleeting and, over time, just broken promises grasping for the wind? We hold on to the belief that looking better, making more money, being out of debt, or becoming successful will fulfill what is lacking and bring us happiness. Even if we do accomplish these things, they don't bring us the satisfaction we are looking for.

Look at King Solomon, who was the richest, wisest, most powerful king of all time. He was favored and feared; yet he, with all his earthly possessions, found no peace or happiness without total surrender to God. The book of Ecclesiastes, written by King Solomon, shows his frustration as he acquired and conquered all things, and yet nothing satisfied him.

Making resolutions is not a bad thing, especially if we follow through. But do they bring us closer to God? So, what should our resolutions be as we begin a New Year? We should seek a deeper relationship with our Lord Jesus Christ! This happens through prayer, reading of Scripture, and listening to those that teach the word of God. We should seek a Bible-based church and commit to following the life of Jesus Christ. He alone will bring whatever we are lacking.

He gives us the will and strength to perfect our body, mind, spirit, and soul. We follow Him and turn against sin, asking for health, blessings, and serenity. In obedience, we pledge to tithe our "first fruits," knowing that through His law of reciprocity, there will be financial favor, and all our needs will be met. We will have abundance! We admit our weaknesses, for in Him we are strong! We pledge to simplify our lives and promise to obey Him. We bring all of our needs before Him.

Today, when I seek Him first and foremost, my resolutions and promises become easier to accomplish.

Once I commit to time each day strengthening my relationship with Him, it will multiply the time I have. Just as tithing multiplies my riches! I can ask anything in His name, and it will be given to me.

Philippians 4:13, NKJV

I can do all things through Christ who strengthens me.

Philippians 4:6, NKJV

Be anxious for nothing, but in everything by prayer and supplication, with thanksgiving, let your request be made known to God

A Word is Dead Once It's Been Said (Mr. Little, My 8th Grade English Teacher!)

Keep your tongue from evil, and your lips from speaking deceit.

—Psalm 34:13, NKJV

Most of us do not recognize the power of the tongue and the damage it can cause. Our speech breathes life into our words, putting them out there permanently. It is crazy how something so small can spark a great fire and be so dangerous!

One of our biggest regrets can be how we've wounded others through our unguarded words. But it's not just others we hurt, it also grieves and hurts our Heavenly Father. For some of us, it is extremely difficult to think before we speak. If we will just take a few seconds to understand the effect of our words, we could avoid the irrevocable damage they cause.

Why say anything if it has no benefit, and more importantly, why put negative thoughts and energy out into the universe that can never be taken back?

"If you have nothing good to say, then say nothing at all!" There is simply no confusion in this statement; we must control our tongue. We need to guard what we say to other people.

Today, Father, please give me power over my tongue and help me stop the damage it may cause. Let the Holy Spirit take control of my words before I speak them. Help me stop, listen, and think, *What would Jesus say, what should I say?* For it is in His name I pray, please don't let me say words I regret and can never take back, as well as remember that a word is dead once it's been said.

James 1: 19-20, NKJV

So then, my beloved brethren, let every man be swift to hear, slow to speak, slow to wrath, for the wrath of man does not produce the righteousness of God.

James 3:8, NKJV

But no man can tame the tongue. It is an unruly evil, full of deadly poison.

James 3:6, NKJV

And so, the tongue is a fire, a world of iniquity... and sets on fire the course of nature, and it is set on fire by hell.

I Will Not Live in Sin But in Victory!

For whatever is born of God overcomes the world. And this is the victory that has overcome the world – our faith.
—I John 5:4, NKJV

Victory of sin is found exclusively in the cross. This is the message that sets us free! We don't have to live in a daily struggle. When we start living for Christ and following His footsteps, we will be victorious!

When we become new in Christ, sin will stop making expression through our lives and we become less and less of who we once were. We cannot avoid the nature of sin, but we can learn to deal with and conquer the temptation of sin by holiness, the true evidence of Christianity.

When we don't follow the true doctrine of God's Word and go astray, we can't find "victory over sin and death." Instead, we engage in spiritual warfare. Warfare is the direction of our mind and the object of our faith. It takes us one of two ways, closer to our Heavenly Father or away from Him and into a life of sin.

Everything outside of the message of faith is outside of the message of God and living a Godly life. There is no victory that is *not* of God. The *only* means of victory over sin is by asking for forgiveness and leaving all of our transgressions at the cross.

Today, I live in victory and conquer sin and death through my faith. This faith comes from my personal relationship with Jesus, built on hearing, reading, and knowing His Word. Father protect me from spiritual warfare and the enemy. I will not live in sin but in victory through Christ Jesus!

Romans 6:23, NKJV

For the wages of sin is death, but the gift of God is eternal life in Christ Jesus our Lord.

Psalms 119: 1-8, NKJV

Blessed are the undefiled in the way, who walk in the law of the Lord! Blessed are those who keep His testimonies, who seek Him with the shole heart! They also do no iniquity; they walk in His ways. You have commanded us to keep your precepts diligently. Oh, that my ways were directed to keep Your statutes! Then I would not be ashamed. When I look into all Your commandments. I will praise You with uprightness of heart, when I learn Your righteous judgments. I will keep Your statues; Oh, do not forsake me utterly.

John 14:1-4, NKJV

Let not your heart be troubled; you believe in God, believe also in Me. In My Father's house are many mansions, if it were not so, I would have told you. I go to prepare a place for you. And if I go and prepare a place for you, I will come again and receive you to Myself; that where I am, there you may be also. And where I go you know, and the way you know.

Do I Choose Immediate Gratification or Eternal Peace?

But God forbid that I should boast except in the cross of our Lord Jesus Christ, by whom the world has been crucified to me and I to the world.

—Galatians 6:14, NKJV

We live in a time where "religious" messages are designed to make us feel good about ourselves. We are told that finding "our inner-purpose" brings happiness and contentment. People are teaching the body is the temple, and we should serve the "self." They are great story tellers and deliver messages that are entertaining, often humorous, and leave us with feelings of elation. This is false doctrine, and we need to be very careful not to follow. SELF, self, self is not a message from God, but from Satan.

Satan challenged the sovereignty of God believing he was greater than God and entitled to his own kingdom. He was self-righteous and self-serving and refused to serve anyone but himself. He was banned from Heaven but his fight for control continues. Satan disguises himself as a beacon of light and draws us in when we're not paying attention, and we need to watch and listen carefully.

Self-righteousness will lead us down that path of destruction, going against the teachings of Jesus and into a life of sin. We must have our guard up against the damnable sin of self-righteousness. The focus on "self" keeps us from seeing our need for the Gospel. It leads us to believe the lie we can be good enough (in ourselves) to enter the gates of heaven, and thus, we do not need a Savior who paid the penalty for our sins.

There is only ONE discipline, ONE message, ONE purpose; that is the atonement of the cross and the death and resurrection of our Lord! If the focus is on our own works, we go against Jesus. We cannot serve two masters for there is only one. There is no salvation without total surrender to what Jesus has done for us.

If we are in total alignment with the gospel of Jesus Christ, we are dead to worldliness and self. When we are confident on what the Lord did for us on the cross, our old life is crucified with Him.

Today, I live with amazing grace of God in me and experience the ease of hearing Him speak to me. I claim the supernatural experience of sharing in the atonement and fulfilling of His purpose, not mine. I will not follow doctrine that teaches self-righteousness and self-fulfillment. I will follow the life of Jesus Christ, striving for sanctification through Him. I claim the righteousness of our Lord and Savior and will serve Him with humility and grace.

Ephesians 1:20, NKJV

For by grace you have been saved through faith, and not of yourselves; it is the gift of God, not of works, lest anyone should boast.

1 Timothy 4:1-2, NKJV

Now the Spirit expressly says that in latter times some will depart from the faith, giving heed to deceiving spirits and doctrines of demons, speaking lies in hypocrisy, having their own conscience seared with a hot iron.

The Devil Made Me Do It!

For my people are foolish. They have not known Me, and they have no understanding. They are wise to do evil. But to do good, they have no knowledge.

—Jeremiah 4:22, NKJV

There are three ways in which temptation manifests itself: the world, the flesh, or the devil. But none can affect us without our cooperation. It is easy to blame the devil, but in fact, he can only tempt us; there is no one to blame when we stray from God but ourselves. We can't be saints if sin is in our life. There is no gray area here.

When we look at others who do not know Jesus Christ and see their lives are bountiful, it's hard to reconcile. God gave us free will and allows us to choose our paths. Sinners can have a life of wealth and pleasure, but it is fleeting. We can't be envious of those who choose their riches here on earth. There will be a judgement day and all of the success, power and money in the world won't buy salvation.

The book of Luke, Chapter 16 tells of a rich man and a beggar. When they both died, the beggar went to Heaven, the rich man went to Hell (Hades). The rich man seeing the beggar (Lazarus) from afar sitting with Abraham, called out for mercy, first for himself and then for his five brothers still living on earth. But Abraham answered that he and his brothers had the opportunity to know the Word but chose not to follow. God chastens those who know.

We all are given the opportunity to repent. It will just be harder for the man who is wealthy and serves money first. The enemy knows that wealth is a great temptation for man and will use it to lead him away from God. The rich man counts his blessings here on earth, but the poor man seeks the kingdom and blessings in Heaven.

Today, I acknowledge there is no promise that life will be easier for the saints or have less temptation. In fact, quite the contrary. Jesus warns us we will be persecuted in His name and tempted by the enemy to move away from God and towards the riches here on earth. This is my choice. I live for the death of Christ and the death of my humanly body and will sacrifice all things to be with Him for eternity. I choose to turn from sin and seek repentance and salvation. I will serve and glorify Him for all of my days, here on earth.

Proverbs 3:12, NKJV

"For whom the Lord Loves he corrects, just as a father, the son in whom he delights."

Luke 18:24, NKJV

"How hard it is for those who have riches to enter the kingdom of God!"

James 1:14

But each one is tempted when he is drawn away by his own desires and enticed.

Don't Let Jealosy Rear Its Ugly Head!

You shall not covet your neighbor's house; you shall not covet your neighbor's wife, nor his male servant, nor his female servant, nor his ox, nor his donkey, nor anything that is your neighbor's.

—Exodus 20:17, NKJV

The Tenth Commandment makes clear the Lord forbids the sin that no one sees – our jealous thoughts and desires that long for what belongs to others. We fail to keep His law when our hearts are filled with jealous discontent; specifically, this commandment is about sins of the heart. When you look at other sins, murder, adultery, theft, and idolatry, they are all rooted in jealous discontent; when we covet what others have.

It was jealousy that caused Lucifer and one third of the angels to fall and be banished from God for all eternity. Adam and Eve coveted God's knowledge and ate the forbidden fruit, banishing mankind from the Garden of Eden. It grieves God's heart when we are filled with envy. When we are coveting what others have, we are reflecting discontentment and ungratefulness. God made each of us unique with our own special gifts and blessings, and He wants us to be thankful for all that we possess. The answer to covetousness is not the absence of all desire, but rather the cultivation of contentment.

We must learn to be content in every circumstance, resisting jealousy or yearning of what we are lacking. We should endeavor to be grateful to God for every blessing He has given to us; only then will we be less inclined to covet that which is not ours. Jealousy reflects an unrepentant heart. The true believer knows that God has given us everything according to His plan, and we lack for nothing.

Today, let me be thankful to the Lord for the blessings I possess. I will not be jealous of my brother or sister and covet what is not mine. I am content in every circumstance, and I express my gratitude to my Heavenly Father for making me perfect in His eyes.

Mark 7:20-23, NKJV

And He [Jesus] said, "What comes out of a man that defiles a man. For from within, out of the heart of men, proceed evil thoughts, adulteries, fornications, murders, thefts, covetousness, wickedness, deceit, lewdness, an evil eye, blasphemy, pride, foolishness. All these evil things come from within and defile a man."

Micah 2: 1-2, NKJV

Woe to those who devise iniquity and work out evil on their beds! At morning light, they practice it, because it is in the power of their hand. They covet fields and take them by violence, also houses, and seize them. So, they oppress a man and his house, a man and his inheritance.

Hebrews 13: 5, NKJV

Let your conduct be without covetousness; be content with such things as you have. For He Himself has said, 'I will never leave you nor forsake you.'

A Smiling Face

*A merry heart makes a cheerful countenance [face], but by
sorrow of the heart the spirit is broken.*
                                        —Proverbs 15:13, NKJV

A smiling face is an Earth-like star,
A frown can't bring out the beauty that you are;
Love within, and you'll begin smiling;
There are brighter days ahead.
Don't mess your face up with better tears,
Cause life is gonna be what it is;
It's okay, please don't delay from smiling
There are brighter days ahead.
A smiling face you don't have to see,
cause it's as joyful as a Christmas tree/
Love within and you'll begin smiling;
There are brighter days ahead.
Love's not competing/ it's on your side.
You're in life's picture, so why must you cry:
So, for a friend, please begin to smile, please;

There are brighter days ahead.
—Stevie Wonder; "Smile Please"

Smiling has long been associated with well-being and an overall sense of life satisfaction. The saying, "Smile and the world smiles with you" is also true. If you give someone a smile, it is very rare that they don't smile back. People who smile have also been linked to looking and feeling younger. Studies have shown people who are always smiling have more friends, more successful careers, and live longer.

Often seen as a pleasant or encouraging appearance, a smile can lift our spirits and others. When we are feeling down or depressed, if we put on a smile, it actually elevates our mood. A smile depicts a joyful, happy spirit; trusting that God is *the source* for our hope and happiness. We should find comfort that He desires all of His Children to live in peace and contentment. Someone who is in God's good grace will find happiness and be able to share it with others. The fact that He is always present and there for us, should bring happiness and keep a smile on our face!

Today, I will share a smile with a stranger. My smile represents the joy I feel inside, as a believer and follower of Jesus Christ. I smile to show my Heavenly Father my gratitude and happiness. I thank you Father, for You are my reason to smile!

Romans 15:13, NKJV

Now may the God of hope fill you with all joy and peace in believing, that you may abound in hope by the power of the Holy Spirit.

Psalms 144:15, NKJV

Happy are the people whose God is the LORD.

Matthew 6:16, NKJV

Whenever you fast, do not put on a gloomy face as the hypocrites do, for they neglect their appearance so that they will be noticed by men when they are fasting. Truly I say to you, they have their reward in full.

I Can Never Be Good Enough!

The centurion answered and said, "Lord, I am not worthy that You should come under my roof, but only speak a word and my servant will be healed."

—Matthew 8:8, NKJV

The fallacy that we can never be good enough is something the enemy starts whispering in our ears the first second we make the choice of following Christ. The devil tells us we are unworthy of God's love and that we can never do enough to be accepted into His Kingdom. We all struggle with this, trying to overcompensate and over-complicate what it means to be a Christian.

We constantly set goals that are too far to reach and set ourselves up for failure and feelings of guilt, believing we've fallen short of God's expectations for His children.

The only thing necessary to be saved is to profess that Jesus is our Lord and Savior, acknowledge He died for our sins, rose again in three days, and now sits at the right hand of the Father. When we ask for forgiveness of our sins, we are made whole again. Somehow, we think that doesn't apply to us; that somehow, we need to do so much more, to be included in God's Kingdom. The truth is none of us are good enough to receive God's grace and mercy. Only through the blood of Christ are we able to receive salvation and eternal life. No amount of good works, devout prayers, or absence of sin could ever get us there.

If we allow the enemy to convince us that we aren't worthy of God's love, then we will live a life full of frustration, self-doubt, and depression. We must realize that this gift is available to all of us. Regardless of who we have hurt or the bad things we've done or how many sins we've committed, God waits for all sinners to come to Him. God sees our hearts. When we feel inadequate, He sees humility and yearning. We can rest in what Jesus tells us: "that he who is least of these in the kingdom will be greater than John the Baptist" (Luke 7:28, NKJV). What an awesome promise!

Today, I proclaim that I am a child of God and accept His salvation, even though none of us deserve it! I give thanks to Father God, for it was His sacrifice, not mine, that gives me eternal life. I will not let the enemy whisper in my ear and tell me I am not good enough. I am worthy of God's love and will not allow myself to believe the enemy's lies. I refuse to allow the devil to get me down!

Romans 3:23-24, NKJV

For All have sinned and fall short of the glory of God, being justified freely by His grace through the redemption that is in Christ Jesus.

Romans 6:23, NKJV

For the wages of sin is death, but the gift of God is eternal life in Christ Jesus our Lord.

Matthew 11:11, NKJV

"Assuredly, I say to you, among those born of women there has not risen one greater than John the Baptist; but he who is least in the kingdom of heaven is greater than he."

You Can't Give What You Don't Have

Then one of them, a lawyer, asked Him a question, testing Him, and saying, "Teacher, which is the great commandment in the law:" Jesus said to him, "You shall love the Lord your God with all your heart, with all your soul, and will all your mind. This is the first and great commandment. And the second is like it. You shall love your neighbor as yourself. On these two commandments hang all the Law and the Prophets."
—Matthew 22: 35-40, NKVJ

My biggest struggle in becoming a follower of Jesus Christ and living a sanctified life has been learning to love myself. For most of my life, I have extracted love from others, draining them completely in an attempt to fill the void in my heart. The results have been catastrophic, as I have ruined most relationships and burned the ones who truly loved me. Self-doubt and loathing were always blocking me from giving or receiving love.

Love is a verb, meaning it is an action we take. When we look in the mirror, it's so easy to play the "if only" game: "if only we were better looking, skinnier, smarter, richer." These are all the excuses we make for not being satisfied with who we are. To love yourself is not easy, and I think that more people than not go their entire lives never finding it.

"To love one another as you love yourselves" is the Eleventh Commandment Jesus gives us in the New Testament (Mark 12:31, NKJV). He is commanding us to do both, love ourselves as well as love others. Christ came to this earth loving all people; because He was filled with love for the Father and Himself, He was able to give boundlessly to all.

We can only find true self-love when we accept the love of our Heavenly Father. For He loves us so much, He sacrificed His only Son. He loves us so much; He knows the number of hairs on our head. Our Father's Love is boundless, unconditional, and everlasting. He made us in His own image, but each one completely unique with our own set of gifts. Only when we recognize the deep love He has for us, can we find love for ourselves.

Once this happens, everything in our lives will change forever. Where once we were trying to find love and acceptance through others, we now find in our own hearts. This amazing change in our perspective gives us clarity on just how special we are, and regardless of our own insecurities or shortcomings we see, our Father only sees perfection. It is His perfect love, that once accepted, will fill our hearts, bodies, minds, and souls.

Today, I will learn to love myself as my Heavenly Father loves me. I know that until I learn to love myself, there is nothing for me to give. For all the faults that I see through my own eyes, I know that I am perfect in His eyes. I will share His perfect love with everyone. He made me in His image. In fully accepting self-love, I can go out into the world and do what Jesus has commanded, "Love your neighbor as yourself" (Galatians 5:14, NKJV).

Leviticus 19:18, NKJV

You shall not take vengeance, nor bear any grudge against the children of your people, but you shall love your neighbor as yourself; I am the Lord.

Matthew 19:18, NKJV

"Honor your father and your mother, and, you shall love your neighbor as yourself."

Lighten Up, Would Ya!!!

But instead, joy and gladness, slaying oxen and killing sheep, eating meat and drinking wine: let us eat and drink for tomorrow we die!
—Isaiah 22:13, NKJV

Our loving Father is not all about fire and brimstone. He is the opposite (although He makes His message very clear about unbelievers); God wants us to be full of joy and happiness, to laugh and be merry. Our Father in Heaven wants us to see the humor in life. There are many examples in the Bible that show God has a sense of humor. We can see this in the story of David and Goliath.

Goliath was a giant, and although we don't know exactly, he was most likely nine or ten feet tall. The Philistines had used him as their "great warrior," and would taunt the Israelites to find anyone in their tribes to defeat him. David was very young, of small stature, and a shepherd by trade. He would have been absolutely no consequence for Goliath. I can only imagine the laughter and ridicule when David decided to face this giant. Many before had tried to defeat Goliath to no avail. To see the humor, you must imagine the two of them standing in some sort of arena or battlefield. David would have looked like a tiny child in comparison to Goliath, and anyone in the crowd placing odds would have bet the farm against him!

David, who denied the king's armor to go up against Goliath, stood with nothing but his shepherd clothes, a small sling, and a few rocks. You can almost hear Goliath laughing as David approached. However, what no one else knew other than David was He had God on his side! As the giant barreled towards him, he took out the slingshot, put the stone in it, pulled it back, and shot Goliath right between the eyes. David literally knocked him over and killed him with a single stone. I can only imagine after the shock of what had taken place, there were a few chuckles amongst the Israelites!

We are often told that being a Christian means giving up everything that is fun, and that's just not true. Jesus spent much of His time with sinners, eating, drinking, and being merry. There is nothing scriptural that tells us we must behave in any other manner. God wants us to laugh and have joy in our lives. The only gloom and doom He promises is for the non-believer, and for them the future is not bright. But for those who believe in Jesus Christ as their Lord and Savior, there is joy, contentment, peace, and a light-hearted life now and for eternity. We should all enjoy the here and now with great anticipation of our future.

Today, Father, I will be merry and celebrate my life! I accept the joy and happiness that comes from being a follower of Jesus Christ. Let me see the humor in situations and not take life so seriously. I will learn to laugh more, cry less, and be thankful for my salvation. I will show the world what it means to be a Christian, not a promise of fire and brimstone, but a life full of happiness and laughter.

Ecclesiastes 8:15, NKJV

So, I commended enjoyment, because a man has nothing better under the sun that to eat, drink, and be merry; for this will remain with him in his labor all the days of his life which God gives him under the sun.

Ecclesiastes 3:12, NKJV

I know that nothing is better for them than to rejoice, and to do good in their lives.

The Winning Ticket

And the Lord will deliver me from every evil work and pre-serve me for His heavenly kingdom. To Him be glory forever and ever. Amen!

—2 Timothy 4:18, NKJV

All of us would play the lotto if we were guaranteed the winning ticket. The odds of buying a winning ticket in a state lottery are approximately 1 in 292 million. In fact, lottery ticket sales generate roughly 80 million dollars of revenue annually in the US, as players hope to become the latest person beating the odds and winning a once-in-a-lifetime jackpot. The point being, millions of people buy lotto tickets every day, against all odds of winning.

So, what if someone told you that your odds of winning were 100%? Would you buy a ticket? Unlike the odds of a state lottery, we are guaranteed salvation, which is *free* for anyone who seeks it. All we have to do is ask, and we are promised eternal life, as well as a disease and stress-free perfect body and dwelling in a mansion with streets paved of gold.

When we accept Christ as our Lord and Savior, there is a renewal of mind, body, and spirit that comes with never ending joy, peace, and love. There are no other guarantees in life, nothing simpler or easier to obtain.

When I think about this, it is incomprehensible that anyone in their right mind would turn down this amazing, free gift. Why would you choose darkness over light, sorrow over joy, stress over contentment, or turmoil over peace? When we think about salvation in such simple terms, it begs the question: How could anyone turn down a deal like this?

God gave man free will, the power to choose our destiny, and with this comes a tendency to overcomplicate things. For those who choose salvation, it is difficult to see how something so simple becomes so convoluted. It is our duty as followers of Jesus to bring others to Christ and to simplify the meaning of salvation when we talk about it.

If we are speaking to someone that is very defensive and resistant, they will try to get us away from our message with arguments that can easily get us off point. We must never deviate from the pure and simple answer. If we get defensive or argue it weakens our position, giving the non-believer justification for their arguments. There will be times when we walk away, but we should not be frustrated, because sometimes the person that plants the seed does not reap the harvest. We should keep in mind that the lottery of salvation is 100% win or lose, and it is our duty to help everyone possible be on the winning side.

Today, Father, let me see what my responsibility is as a Christian—that I am to win souls for Christ. After my own salvation, there is nothing more important or critical if I am truly your servant. I will keep the message of salvation and the sinner's prayer simple and refuse to engage in an argument that complicates a very simple matter. Please give me strength and discernment to know when and how to approach a non-believer. If I don't know what to say, may the Holy Spirit fill me with the right words. I have an unlimited number of "winning tickets" to share and will not lose any opportunity to give the ultimate prize: Salvation!

2 Timothy 4:2

Preach the word! Be ready in season and out of season, Convince, rebuke, exhort, with all longsuffering and teaching.

Mark 16:15

And He said to them, "Go into all the world and preach the gospel to every creature."

<u>Romans 10:17</u>

So then faith comes by hearing, and hearing by the word of God.

"It's Not Easy Being Green"
—Kermit the Frog

Then the woman of Samaria said to Him, "How is it that You being a Jew, ask a drink from me, a Samaritan woman? For Jews have no dealings with Samaritans."

—John 4:9, NKJV

We should never judge a book by its cover or another person because of the way they look. A man is not defined by the color of his skin, but by what is in his heart. Black, red, yellow, brown, or white, we are all God's children.

We are not born with prejudice, it is something we learn from parents, as well as our social and cultural environments. Hating someone because they are different from us is not a natural response, but one that's developed over time, and it certainly is not godly.

Over the centuries, each culture has developed what they believe Jesus looks like. If you are American, then Jesus is depicted through pictures and films with auburn or blonde hair and blue eyes. The Mexican Jesus (which is more accurate) has light brown skin and dark brown eyes. Jesus was born in the Middle East and had medium brown skin that would have darkened during his years of ministry, as He was always in the sun. If we were to meet Jesus today, it is most likely that we would refer to him as being something other than white.

During his life, Jesus would have been easily identified as an Israelite with ancestors who were slaves to the Romans. Even though there is a direct lineage to King David, He would not have been recognized as being from royal descent or privilege. Jesus was persecuted in part for being Jewish, and He understood discrimination. He did not see race, color, religion, social status, sex, or disability, but looked to what was important—people's relationships with God. Jesus stood for and supported equality, and He showed this throughout His ministry.

When Jesus spoke to the Samaritan woman at the well, His disciples were shocked, because she was considered a foreigner and not to be associated with. His conversation with her was not based on being female or Samarian but focused on her heart. There is no doubt in my mind that Jesus was showing His disciples not to judge based on the color of someone's skin, their eco-nomic status, sex, race, or religion.

Jesus shared His message and the Gospel with ev-eryone and set Paul in motion to preach to the gentiles (Greeks), who at the time would have been considered "the undesirables." If we are truly followers of Jesus Christ and sanctified through the cross, then we will not judge based on anything superficial. We will love everyone and treat them with the same respect as we expect to be treated.

Today, Father, I will really look within at any preju-dices I hold. Whatever I find of myself that is judgmen-tal or biased, I release to you and pray to be cleansed of this wrong thinking. I will love all people regardless of their race, religion, sex, social status, or disability and share the Gospel with everyone. I pray for healing of racial divides and for this nation that faces cultural revolution. Please purify my heart and the hearts of all believers.

John 4:27, NKJV

And at this point His disciples came, and they marveled that He talked with a woman; yet no one said, "What do You see" or "Why are You talking with her?"

Galatians 3:28, NKJV

There is neither Jew nor Greek, there is neither slave nor free, there is neither male nor female; for you are all one in Christ Jesus.

It's Not Easy Being Green – Lyrics by Jim Henson of *Sesame Street**

> *It's not that easy bein' green*
> *Having to spend each day*
> *The color of the leaves*
> *When I think it could be nicer*
> *Bein' red or yellow or gold*
> *Or something much more colorful like that*
>
> *It's not easy bein' green*
> *It seems you blend in*
> *With so many other ordinary things*
> *And people tend to pass you over*
> *Cause you're not standing out*
> *Like flashy sparkles in the water*
> *Or stars in the sky*
>
> *But green's the color of spring*
> *And green can be cool and friendly like*
> *And green can be big like a mountain*
> *Or important like a river or tall like a tree*

When green is all there is to be
It could make you wonder why
But, why wonder? (why wonder)
I'm green and it'll do fine
It's beautiful. And I think it's what I want to be

*Jim Henson used his platform *Sesame Street* to address social issues and problems that children face in this world. "It's Not Easy Being Green" is a wonderful song speaking to issues on being different. This is such a simple message and song, but it is very thought provoking not just for children, but for everyone. Henson's message is we should never judge others by the color of their skin, nor should we ever be ashamed of who we are and how we look to the world.

We Must Learn to Turn the Other Cheek!

Repay no one evil for evil. Have regard for good things in the sight of all men.

—Romans 12:17, NKJV

We can't keep score when it comes to evil or it will overcome us. Many times, when we feel wronged, the other person(s) has no idea they have hurt us. They may walk away having no idea the damage caused by their words or actions. When we choose to pay back those wrong doings, it hurts us more by perpetuating negativity in our lives. We must turn our pain and anger over to God and His promise to take care of it!

Our natural reaction is to protect ourselves, and when someone harms us intentionally, it is extremely hard not to retaliate. However, if we wait and pray, our

Father in Heaven does seek vengeance for His children. He doesn't want us to live with anger or resentment, because these feelings will open the door for Satan.

We must turn the other cheek, pray for our enemy, and pay back evil with kindness. These things we are told to do by our Heavenly Father. Let God seek our vindication, and we can sit back and watch our enemies fall.

Today, if wronged, I will not seek my own vengeance but wait upon the Lord. It may not be immediate, but He will retaliate against evil and vindicate His children. I choose to pray for my enemies and turn the other cheek. Father, please fill my heart with love, not hate, and help me love those who come against me.

Deuteronomy 32:35, NKJV

Vengeance is Mine, and recompense; Their foot shall slip in due time; For the day of their calamity is at hand, And the things to come hasten upon them.

Romans 12:19, NKJV

Beloved, do not avenge yourselves, but rather give place to wrath; for it is written, "Vengeance is Mine, I will repay," says the Lord.

Getting Rid of Dead Weight

So, they picked up Jonah and threw him into the sea, and the sea ceased from its raging.

—Jonah 1:15, NKJV

Jonah was instructed by the Lord to go to the city of Nineveh and cry out against their wickedness. But out of fear and in disobedience to the Lord, Jonah boarded a ship going the opposite way to Tarshish. Immediately, huge storms broke out, frightening the mariners. Trying to avoid being capsized, they threw the ship's cargo out into the sea. All the men cried out to their gods because they were afraid, and yet the storm did not let up. Then the crew cast lots to determine whose fault it was for the tempestuous storms, and the lot fell on Jonah.

So, the men went to Jonah and asked what was causing the trouble (storms), and when he told them he was a Hebrew and feared the God of Heaven, the men were exceedingly afraid. Soon after, they realized that it was Jonah who had angered the Lord, and they threw him into the sea. Immediately, the storms ceased!

When we are called to travel in one direction and choose to go another, there will be calamity in our lives and for those who are around us. The Lord dealt with Jonah for his disobedience, just as He will deal with us. But what's equally important, is when we go against God, moving in the wrong direction, is the affect it has on the other people in our lives.

The mariners, in their fear for the God of Heaven, were faced with a choice as they traveled down their own path. For they were experiencing God's anger against Jonah, and to shed themselves of this trouble, they got rid of the *dead weight*. Removing the cargo from the ship was not the answer to surviving the storm. Their answer came by throwing Jonah off the ship!

Many times, good people and even our loved ones weigh us down with their bad decisions. If we are true followers of Jesus Christ and walking in the path of righteousness, there will be times we face tough decisions. When we are committed to Christ, then He is first and foremost. Anything or anyone that stands in our way must be tossed out or put aside in our quest to follow Him.

Today, I may lose relationships to perfect my relationship and love for Jesus Christ. This choice will be difficult at first, but the rewards greatly exceed the loss. When moving towards Christ, I recognize the dead weight in my life and what is holding me back from the most important relationship; it is the one I have with my Lord and Savior!

Proverbs 13:20, NKJV

He who walks with wise men will be wise, But the companion of fools will be destroyed.

1 Corinthians 15:33, NKJV

Do not be deceived: "Evil company corrupts good habits."

The Recurring Pattern of Sin

If we confess our sins, He is faithful and just to forgive us our sins and to cleanse us from all unrighteousness.

—I John 1:9, NKJV

We are born into sin. That is why Jesus died on the cross for us. If not, none of us would make it to Heaven. Even the saints cannot live a perfect, sinless life. As we move closer to walking in the footsteps of Jesus, our sins for the most part are minimized, our ability to walk away becomes easier, and recognition of our transgressions clearer.

What we need to focus on as believers is our pattern of recurring sin. Very similar to addiction, we must first be willing to accept our weaknesses, admit we can't break the pattern on our own, and then conquer these transgressions that plague our lives through our relationship with Jesus Christ. A relationship that can only come from knowing the Word of God.

An addict may go to a facility for several months, then to a half-way house, and eventually move back into society, spending the rest of their life avoiding pitfalls. The ones who are successful in beating their addictions participate in ongoing counseling and support groups, with many eventually becoming mentors to other addicts. They face a daily struggle, avoiding their old recurring patterns. There is no final breakthrough, as they will always call themselves a "recovering alcoholic, drug addict or gambler." It's an acceptance they will never be fully recovered, and they must work every day to defeat their addiction.

The person who continues to be defeated by temptation, resulting in recurring sins, also struggles with an addiction. We can and do become addicted to sin. When we finally condemn ourselves for recurring sins, we admit before God our sins and ask for His forgiveness. True confession and repentance bring forth God's immediate grace and a changing of our spirit. But we must realize that once forgiven, the chains that formerly bound us can be broken by our future actions. Like the addict, we must outline a program that brings us closer to Christ, for when we repent, it is for sins past. Our struggle becomes the temptation to repeat our sins in the future.

Today, I commit myself to a daily regimen of prayer and meditation, an allotted time and plan to read the Bible every day. God's Word will increase my understanding of His principles, but also change my behavior, making me stronger and wiser. As my knowledge grows, so will my defenses against sin in the future, and I will no longer be tempted. My identification will change dramatically, for once I was a sinner, but now I am a servant to my Lord through fellowship with Jesus Christ.

Hebrews 10:26-27, NKJV

For if we go on sinning deliberately after receiving the knowledge of the truth, there no longer remains a sacrifice for sins, but a fearful expectation of judgment, and a fury of fire that will consume the adversaries.

Is My Own Self-Righteousness Causing Grief to Jesus?

I delight to do Your will, O my God, and Your law is within my heart.

—Psalms 40:8, NKJV

Anytime we rely on our own will and righteousness, the results of our actions will be disastrous. We can't be self-righteous and help others get on the right path without causing grief, misunderstandings, guilt, or anger. Even if we don't cause harm to others, our stubbornness and self-will grieve the spirit of Jesus Christ. When we rely on self-righteousness and pride, we not only hurt His spirit but persecute Him. We will cause destruction unless we have a perfect spirit of oneness with our Lord.

When Jesus spoke, He always acknowledged His words were from the Father. He never craved the glory but gave the glory to God. Just as He did His Father's will on earth, we too must make sure to do Jesus's will. If we serve Him in a spirit that is not His, then we are pushing our claims of serving Him through the spirit of Satan.

There were many times when His own disciples spoke out of self-righteousness, and Jesus would rebuke them. He totally understood the damage their pride could cause. Jesus spoke with authority and had complete understanding of serving His Father in Heaven. There will never be anyone greater here on Earth than Jesus, and yet He was never self-righteous, nor claimed recognition. Jesus always, with humility and honor, glorified the Father.

Today, I surrender my self-righteousness and pride. Father let me understand that my words and actions are powerful and can grieve the one I love the most, my Lord and Savior, Jesus Christ. When I am given the opportunity to share a message of utmost importance, let me always remember, it is from Him not me. Let me give Him glory, not grief, as His humble servant and follower.

Luke 9:55, NKJV

But He turned and rebuked them and said, "You do not know what manner of spirit you are of."

Philippians 3:9-10, NKJV

...and be found in Him, not having my own righteousness, which is from the law, but that which is through faith in Christ, the righteousness which is from God by faith; that I may know Him and the power of His resurrection from the dead.

Romans 10:3-4, NKJV

For they being ignorant of God's righteousness, and seeking to establish their own righteousness, have not submitted to the righteousness of God. For Christ is the end of the law for righteousness to everyone who believes.

Romans 10:10, NKJV

For with the heart one believes unto righteousness, and with the mouth confession is made unto salvation.

Strife is a Blessing Blocker!

First be reconciled to your brother, and then come and offer your gift.

—Matthew 5:24, NKJV

The definition of strife is a bitter, sometimes violent, conflict or dissension; an act of contention; struggle; exertion of contention for superiority.[8]

If we are angry with a person or circumstance, it causes strife in our life. When we deal with strife, anger, or bitterness, there is no room left for blessings. Strife can also destroy families, friendships, churches, and marriages; it leads to ungodly traits like pride, hate, and jealousy.

Holding a grudge against another will hinder our relationship with the Lord. When we have something against someone, we should kindly and humbly try and approach them directly. It's not always possible to reconcile with the person or situation that we are grieved about, and in those instances the only control for reconciliation within ourselves is through the power of Christ.

However, whenever possible, it is so important to face our situation straight forward, and if there is another person involved, we should go to them quickly and resolve the matter. This, in and of itself, will be a blessing not only for us but also for our brothers and sisters.

Satan loves strife, and he is the match to the fire that will escalate what may be a very small matter into one that is unmanageable. The devil is ready to pounce when anger takes control. It is up to us to never let something go that far. We need to avoid negative feelings from manifesting.

When we surrender time and control to strife, it will fester and grow, overcoming us with negative feelings. These feelings negate good and consume our thoughts, leaving no room to receive blessings from the Lord. Faith is about forgiving and not about who is right and who is wrong. When we let these situations escalate and allow ourselves to be overcome with anger, the reason it started is soon forgotten, but the strife stays with us. Don't let strife internalize and fester but release it immediately before it becomes a blessing blocker.

Today, If I focus on the strife in my life, I lose focus on God. I must learn to capture those thoughts and give them immediately to Him. Control is learning that I have no control, and when I let go, I let God in. Father, please remove the strife that keeps me from Your blessings.

2 Corinthians 10:5, NKJV

"...bringing every thought into captivity to the obedience of Christ."

Proverbs 20:3, NKJV

Avoiding strife brings a man honor, but every fool is quarrelsome.

Proverbs 13:10, NKJV

By pride comes nothing but strife, but with the well-advised is wisdom.

2 Timothy 2:23, NKJV

But avoid foolish and ignorant disputes, knowing that they generate strife.

Who is My Neighbor?

And he, wanting to justify himself, said to Jesus, "And who is my neighbor?"

—Luke 10:29, NKJV

There was a certain lawyer wanting to test Jesus, and he said, "Who is my neighbor?" As often was the case, Jesus answered with a parable and told him of the Good Samaritan (Luke 10:30-35, NKJV). When finished, Jesus asked who the lawyer thought was the neighbor in the story, and he answered, "He who showed mercy on him" (Luke 10:37, NKJV).

A neighbor is not our family (that we are born in to) or our friends (that we choose), but everyone else we encounter in our lives. They are strangers, yet the Bible tells us to love them.

Paul tells us, "and if there is any other commandment, all are summed up in this saying... to love your neighbor" (Romans 13:9, NKJV).

Of course, this is easier said than done. In this fast-paced world, we don't often know our neighbor, and we may have never gotten past the casual greeting or hello. How do we find the time to love that person? What if we have different beliefs, affiliations, lifestyles—or maybe after sharing time, we just don't like them?

This is exactly when we must look beyond the self, let go of prejudices and prejudgments, and look to our Father in Heaven, remembering who we are and who we serve. For every man and woman on Earth is created in His image, and we must remove the blinders of our own experiences to view *all people* through the eyes of Christ. We cannot know the burdens our neighbors have carried, or what circumstances make them different from us. As a follower of Jesus Christ, we must approach our neighbors with love and acceptance, and not judgement or rejection.

Today, I ask myself, "What purpose is served if I only love those close to me?" Jesus spent His time with tax collectors, prostitutes, and sinners for a reason; these were the people that needed Him the most. Father, please give me the heart to love my neighbor and reach beyond those in my inner circle, just as Christ loved *all*, including the sinners.

Leviticus 19:18, NKJV

...But You shall love your neighbor as yourself; I am the Lord.

Romans 13:9, NKJV

...and if there is any other commandment, are all summed up in this saying, namely, "You shall love your neighbor as yourself."

Mark 12:31, NKJV

And the second, like it, is this: "You shall love your neighbor as yourself. There is no other commandment greater than these."

Valentine's Day...A Day to Share My Love!

Love never fails.

—1 Corinthians 13:8, NKJV

The exact origins and identity of Saint Valentine are unclear. Legend has it Valentine was a priest under the rule of Claudius the Cruel, who banned marriages and engagements in Rome around the year 278 A.D. Realizing the injustice, the priest continued to marry young lovers in secret until the Emperor discovered his actions and sentenced him to death. It is said these orders to cut off Valentine's head were carried out on February 14th.

Stories vary as to how the martyr's name became associated with romance; however, some believe the date of his death may have been mangled with the Feast of

Lupercalia, a pagan festival of love. However, it is a fact that in 496 A.D., Pope Gelasius put an end to the Feast of Lupercalia and declared that February 14th be celebrated as St. Valentine's Day.

If this legend is true, then, as in so many great movements of the past, one person with one idea and the boldness to share it affected history! What if each one of us decided today, "I will not only share my love with those closest to me but include one more person, someone I barely know or even a stranger." In the frame of "paying it forward," it is unimaginable what kind of movement this could start, and what better message could there be than LOVE!!!

Who is the person in my office that never gets flowers or the neighbor that just lost their spouse? Who is the woman that sits alone every Sunday during Church service, or what about the person that greets me every morning as I stop to buy coffee? Or the one I see in the elevator that always looks sad? The possibilities are endless! What if today, when I am purchasing a gift for my loved ones, I grab one more and give it to a stranger. I could tell someone that Jesus loves them, and I love them. Could I save someone from thoughts of depression or even suicide as they face this day feeling no one loves them? Maybe I am the one who is alone today. How much brighter would my day be if I extended an act of kindness?

Today, I will start my own movement to fulfil what Scripture tells us: *Love your neighbor as yourself!* I will show my love to a stranger and expect nothing in return, get out of my comfort zone and pursue finding someone who is alone and sad. I will celebrate Saint Valentine, not only on February 14th, but every day, by sharing God's love!

1 Corinthians 13:13, NKJV

And now abide faith, hope, love, these three; but the greatest of these is love.

Romans 12:10, NKJV

Be kindly affectionate to one another with brotherly love, in honor giving preference to one another.

Solus Christus— There is Only ONE Way!

I am the way, the truth, and the life, No one comes to the Father except through me.

—John 14:6, NKJV

We are faced with perilous times when, in the last few decades, some of the biggest religious institutions founded on Christianity have opened their doctrines to the possibility that there may be more than one way to achieve eternal life. For this very reason, after forty-five years, being baptized and having joyfully served my church, I denounced my association with this denomination. Before leaving, I met with the pastor, expressing my deep concerns. Sadly, he said that due to the financial reliance, our church could not afford to take a stand against the National Alliance. This shook me to my core! How can you stand for Christianity if you remove Christ as the Savior and Son of God?

Unfortunately, they are joined with many other "religions" who have taken this non-biblical stance, not only about salvation, but other core issues all questioning the validity of Scripture.

We should run, not walk from religions that want to please the masses for their own gain and who have been blinded by greed, completely losing their way. They compromise the whole reason their church was founded, to spread the good news of salvation through God's only begotten son, Jesus Christ.

Today, I recognize it is my responsibility to make sure I hear the word of the Holy Bible and follow the message of Christ. For even if it is another who leads me astray through false doctrine, it is *my salvation* that is at stake! There is nothing, not one shred of evidence in the Bible suggesting there is any other way except through Jesus Christ for me to receive salvation and eternal life. As His follower, it is my duty to support and attend a church that teaches biblical principles. I will live as a true Christian and follower of Jesus Christ, never adding or taking away from the Word of the living God.

John 3;18, NKJV

"For he who believes in Him is not condemned; but he who does not believe is condemned already, because he has not believed in the name of the only begotten Son of God."

Psalms 78: 36-37, NKJV

"Nevertheless, they flattered Him with their mouth, and they lied to Him with their tongue; For their heart was not steadfast with Him, nor were they faithful in His covenant.

1 Timothy 2:5, NKJV

"For there is one God and one Mediator between God and men, the Man Christ Jesus..."

Luke 21:8, NKJV

"Take heed that you not be deceived."

God is Big Enough!

Behold, I will bring it health and healing; I will heal them and reveal to them the abundance of peace and truth. And I will cause the captives of Judah and the captives of Israel to return and will rebuild those places as at the first. I will cleanse them from all their iniquity by which they have sinned against Me, and I will pardon all their iniquities by which they have sinned and by which they have transgressed against me.
—Jeremiah 33: 6-8, NKJV

Our Heavenly Father is in the restoration business. He restores our health, relationships, financial situations, and nations. There is nothing too big for Him. Regardless of how bad we mess things up or when we think our actions have caused irrevocable damage, He will make us whole again.

The act of restoring is renewal, revival, or reestablishment. It is the return of something to a former, original, normal, or unimpaired condition; a restitution of something taken away or lost.

The biblical meaning of the word "restoration" is to receive back more than has been lost to the point where the final state is greater than the original condition. The main point is that someone or something is improved beyond measure. Repeatedly throughout the Bible, God blesses people for keeping faith through hardships, by making up for their losses and giving them more than they previously had.

When we destroy something, intentional or not, we are riddled with guilt and regret. Often, we cause devastation to those we love the most and are left feeling helpless to repair the damages. We are so blessed that we have a God who is big enough to restore what we have destroyed, no matter how big or small. If we repent, submit ourselves to our Heavenly Father, admit what we have done and ask for forgiveness, He will not only restore what we have torn down, but repair the damages beyond anything we can imagine.

Today, I repent for all of the damage caused by my actions. Please, Father, restore what I have destroyed and forgive me for the hurt and anguish I have caused others. You are the God of salvation and restoration. I am thankful there is nothing too big for You.

Psalms 85:4, NKJV

Restore us, O God of our salvation, and cause Your anger toward us to cease.

Lamentations 5:19-22, NKJV

You, O lord, remain forever; Your throne from generation to generation. Why do You forget us forever, and forsake us for so long a time? Turn us back to You, O Lord, and we will be restored; Renew our days as of old, unless You have utterly rejected us, and are very angry with us!

Zachariah 9:12 NKJV

Return to the stronghold, you prisoners of hope. Even today I declare that I will restore double to you.

Seeking Righteousness— Making the Right Choices

Blessed are those who hunger and thirst for righteousness, for they shall be filled.

—Matthew 5:6, NKJV

We all know basic right from wrong, and yet so many of us still choose to do the wrong thing. Every minute of every day, we are all faced with choices. The slightest of these may not change the outcome of our lives, but the big ones can. That's why we must seek righteousness in everything that we do.

Hindsight is always 20/20, and all of us have made bad choices and seen the consequences of those decisions. Unfortunately, there are no "re-do's" in life; we can't go back and undo our bad choices. However, we can learn from them and avoid repeating mistakes in the future. If we seek the kingdom of God in His righteousness, it changes our perspective and moving forward, changes us within.

When we start thinking, *"What would Jesus do,"* it changes our mindset, and our decisions to make the right choice will become easier. We will start to recognize there is only one right way each time we are faced with a choice, and that is *His* way.

As we seek and accept salvation, then all of our past bad choices are not only forgiven, but also corrected in our new lives. The past is forgotten, and the future looks so bright! We can rely on the Holy Spirit that dwells within us to guide and lead us in every decision. Our bad decisions will diminish when we seek righteousness, and our paths will be straightened and much easier than before.

Today, I will look within and ask, "Do I serve with the humility of Jesus Christ? Do I hunger and thirst for righteousness?" Father, please give me humility as I seek to live a righteous life. Let me make the right choices and learn from all of the wrong choices I have made. Let me show the world what it means to serve You as You lead me down that path of righteousness.

2 Corinthians 5:21, NKJV

For He made Him who knew no sin to be sin for us, that we might become the righteousness of God in Him.

Proverbs 2:20, NKJV

So, you may walk in the way of goodness, and keep to the paths of righteousness.

Psalms 25: 4-5, NKJV

Show me Your ways, O Lord; Teach me Your paths. Lead me in Your truth and teach me, For you are the God of my salvation; On You I wait all the day.

We Can Give the Gift of Eternal Life

The race is not to the swift, nor the battle to the strong, nor bread to the wise, nor riches to men of understanding, nor favor to men of skill; but time and chance happen to them all. For man also does not know his time; like fish taken in a cruel net, like birds caught in a snare, so the sons of men are snared in an evil time, when it falls suddenly upon them.
—Ecclesiastes 9:11-12, NKJV

For those who do not believe that Christ died for us on the cross, there is only one life and one death here on Earth. The unbeliever is scared of disease and death because for them life on earth is all there is, and they have no promise of eternity. When we share the message of salvation it is important to share what we know to be true, but also why it is true.

When an unbeliever tries to reconcile evolution with creation and things like the age of Earth, it can be confusing. It is so important as believers that we can address the theory of evolution and be able to defend creation. Scripture tells us that God is infinite in all things. When we grasp the concept of infinity, then it is easier to comprehend that the Earth is millions of years old. For our maker, seven days could be seven thousand years in Man's time. Knowing this, we can explain creation. We take comfort that God is the Creator of all things but can't take for granted that everyone else understands this.

Fear of the unknown, when we are witnessing to others, is an opening for us to share the gospel. When we can offer someone the opportunity for eternal life, we will get their attention. That is what we know as Christians. The why is being able to clearly define how our beliefs are possible.

Today, I thank You, Father, for giving me eternal life through the sacrifice of Your only begotten Son. For we know that once we become a follower of Jesus Christ, we will never perish, but have everlasting life. I ask that you give me the opportunity to speak with unbelievers and help them reconcile evolution versus creation. Help me bring them to Christ and give them the gift of eternal life!

Ecclesiastes 2:11, NKJV

He has made everything beautiful in its time. Also, He has put eternity in their hearts, except that no one can find out the work that God does from beginning to end.

1 John 2:17, NKJV

And the world is passing away, and the lust of it; but he who does the will of God abides forever.

Science Versus Scripture

He is the image of the invisible God, the firstborn over all creation. For by Him all things were created that are in heaven and that are on earth, visible, and invisible, whether thrones or dominions or principalities or powers. All things were created through Him and for Him. And He is before all things, and in Him all things consist.

—Colossians 1:15-17, NKJV

The first book of the Bible was written almost 5,000 years ago. What was true about God's Word in the beginning will be true until the end of time. The truth of Scripture becomes stronger with time, as prophesies are tested, studied, and fulfilled. The truth dissected again and again will always have the same result and answer. It is the living Word of God.

What the body of Christ must recognize is science can be compared to so many religions that have come and gone. Each declaring a "new or better way" to receive eternal life and purpose. Jesus warned us of "coming prophets and false preaching" that will lead us astray. When the truth is revealed and the light shines on these new theories, they either fall apart or support the living word of God!

Mankind was born with an inquisitive mind and has been searching for answers on the "chicken or egg" theory since the beginning of time. When looking at science, there have been theories set forth throughout time. Some have been proven, and there are many that have been disproven. Up to a few hundred years ago, people believed the world was flat and the sun traveled around the earth. People thought Christopher Columbus was crazy! But what is amazing about Columbus is his belief that the world was round was based on Scripture, and by faith he discovered the New World.

Think about growing up and being taught about evolution. How easy it was to accept we evolved from monkeys. And yet Darwin's theory has proved over time to be false, just as believing the world was flat and that Columbus was going to sail to the end of the earth and fall off.

For centuries, science believed that man's life was totally dependent and sustained by air. It has now been proven that the human body is sustained by blood. We will die after a certain amount of time without air, but we cannot live without blood. This is significant to believers in relation to being washed by the blood of Christ. Blood is life, and through the shedding of His blood, we receive a new life.

There are scientists who have recently discovered and believe there is a part of our brain that exists independently of our bodies. Their "theory" is that part of the brain (our souls) leaves the dead body and moves to another living being. This scientific theory validates stories of people who have died and been resuscitated and reported "feelings of being above the body and looking down," just prior to coming back to life and in their own bodies. They support the idea of reincarnation or extra-terrestrial beings as to where this entity goes, but we know the soul goes one of two places immediately after death.

Science continues to prove everything God tells us is true, supporting our faith in God's word. Scripture has, and forever will, stand the test of time. The Bible is truth, and the message is eternal. God is the Alpha and the Omega, the beginning and the end, and the Almighty Scientist and Creator.

Today, I will study the Word, and see that God is the Almighty Scientist and Creator. I acknowledge that every answer to science is held in scripture. I claim God's Word as the truth and reconcile that science and scripture do co-exist. Lord, please give me the opportunity to speak to supporters of evolution and other false theories. Help me, through knowledge of Your Word, bring them to Christ.

Daniel 12:4, NKJV

But you, Daniel, shut up the words, and seal the book until the time of the end; may shall run to and fro, and knowledge shall increase.

Genesis 1:1-3, NKJV

In the beginning God created the heavens and the earth. The earth was without form, and void; and darkness was on the face of the deep. And the Spirit of God was hovering over the face of the waters. Then God said, "let there be light"; and there was light.

Ecclesiastes 1:13, NKJV

And I set my heart to seek and search out by wisdom concerning all that is done under heaven; this burdensome task God has given to the sons of man, by which they may be exercised.

A God-Fearing Man

Blessed is the man who fears the Lord, who delights greatly in His commandments.

—Psalms 112:1, NKJV

The book of Psalms, chapter 112 gives a very thorough description of a God-fearing man. It highlights ten key points that dictate what a man should be: he lives and exhibits a life of honor. He is financially responsible. He is a role model to other men. He is a leader. He strives for holiness. He is outwardly kind and cares for others. He is mature beyond reproach and desires great levels of spirituality and growth. He is watchful over his family and aware of his God-given role. He clearly demonstrates love, and he is not contentious, but appreciates peace. The Word of God is his foundation.

All of this sounds simple enough, but in reality, there is so much confusion and societal distractions in our world today. It forces men to walk a fine line, leaning on God's guidance to fulfill his role as a leader while avoiding accusations of being a chauvinist by society. This pressure can easily pull Him away from God's instructions and cause feelings of failure or discontentment and spiritual separation. A man must stay firm in his faith, be called back to purity, and walk with God.

In the book of James chapter 1, verse 8, we are reminded that a "double-minded man is unstable in all ways." A god-fearing man must be steadfast and stand strong against the enemy. He must ignore the pressures from the secular world. Godly men should stand up against outside pressures and be held accountable.

Today, I pray for men to have the courage and strength to be the leader of their household. I lift up my brother, father, husband or child to live according to God's commands. I give thanks to my heavenly Father for giving instruction on what a God-fearing man looks like, and in times of weakness, may he go to God's word to find strength and guidance.

1 Timothy 5:8, NKJV

But if anyone does not provide for his own, and especially for those of his household, he has denied the faith and is worse than an unbeliever.

Proverbs 27:17, NKJV

As iron sharpens iron, so a man sharpens the countenance of his friend.

232

1 Corinthians 13:11, NKJV

When I was a child, I spoke as a child, I understood as a child. I thought as a child; but when I became a man, I put away childish things.

A Righteous Woman

Who can find a virtuous wife? For her worth is far above rubies. The heart of her husband safely trusts her; so, he will have no lack of gain. She does him good and not evil all the days of her life...But a woman who fears the Lord, she shall be praised. Give her of the fruit of her hands, and let her own works praise her in the gates.

—Proverbs 31: 10-31, NKJV

According to the biblical account, King Solomon had 700 wives and 300 concubines. In reading the entire chapter of Proverbs 31, I have often joked that his description of a virtuous wife must have been a culmination of all of his wives! Can one woman be all of these things? Joking aside, it is believed by some Old Testament scholars that the author of Proverbs 31 was most likely Solomon, and the writings were about his mother, Bathsheba. Regardless, there are a few points to take away from this chapter that are important to a woman striving to be godly and righteous.

First and foremost, God knows that man is dependent on a woman to live a sanctified, holy life. It also shows her to be the head of the household, a partner to her husband, and an integral part to his success. Another very important part that has been lost in today's society is how important it is for a woman to keep the family unit intact.

Since Ruth Ginsburg unified women in the fight against gender discrimination and inadvertently started the women's liberation movement, working at home has become controversial, and in many cases frowned upon. The women's lib movement has been the downfall of society and the reason for so much dissatisfaction amongst women. It has also led to the demise of marriage and family.

The pressure on women to mark their place in society and the work force has overshadowed the role of wife and mother, leaving women with feelings of unworthiness for leading the biblical role that God commands of her.

This is a subject so close to my heart, having gone through divorce when my son was only four. I was forced back into the workplace, and it was my child who suffered. Not all of us have a choice in this matter, and we do what we can. I chose a career and independence over being the best possible wife to my husband and mother to my son. I have lived to regret it. What I didn't understand then, that I certainly know now, is being a stay-at-home mom is more important than any career. There is no greater responsibility than to raise children to live a sanctified life. My prayers for addressing this subject is it helps other women from moving away from our Father's instructions for being a good wife and mother.

Father, I pray for all of the mothers that are struggling to balance everything and live as a righteous woman. Please give them the strength to follow your commands and surround them with people who uplift them and commend what they do. Let every man who is married to a godly woman fully appreciate her and what she means to him and their children. God bless the mother, daughter, and wife, and let them see the difference they make in our lives.

Genesis 2:18, NKJV

And the Lord God said, "It is not good that man should be alone; I will make him a helper comparable to him."

Titus 2: 3-5, NKJV

The older women likewise, that they be reverent in behavior, not slanderers, not given to much wine, teachers of good things, that they admonish the young women to love their husbands, to love their children, to be discreet, chaste, home-

makers, good, obedient to their own husbands, that the word of God may not be blasphemed.

Galatians 3:28, NKJV

There is neither Jew nor Greek, there is neither slave nor free, there is neither male nor female; for you are all one in Christ Jesus.

Who Am I to Judge???

He who is without sin among you, let him throw a stone at her first.

—John 8:7, NKJV

Jesus tells us in the eighth chapter of John why we shouldn't judge others. The scribes and Pharisees brought a woman who had been caught in adultery to Jesus. The punishment for adultery according to the laws of Moses was that the accused be stoned to death. They were testing Jesus by bringing this woman who had clearly sinned, so they might have something of which to accuse Him. Jesus knowing all, including what the Pharisees were thinking, said, "He who is without sin among you, let him throw a stone at her first" (John 8:7, NKJV). His message was crystal clear: We are all sinners and have no right to stand in judgement.

There is only one without sin, and therefore the *only one* who can (and will) ever pass judgement.

Jesus tells us plainly that if we judge others, we too will be judged. We are to leave judgement up to Him. Yet we live in a society that has drawn a fine line between spiritual and social judgement. Everywhere we turn, there are tabloids, magazine articles, and television shows that exploit human and social behavior. It has become easy for us to get on the bandwagon and condemn what we see as bad social behavior. This has become painfully clear when we participate in the exploitation of celebrities, politicians, the rich and famous, and the attack by social media to sensationalize their lives. As Christians, we must recognize that any judgement that does not come from God is wrong.

So, if we witness our brother or sister sinning against God, hurting others or themselves, or walking in darkness, what should we do? Gently, with loving kindness and removing all judgement, expose privately to them what we see and express our concern for the damage they may be causing to themselves and others. When we do approach our brother or sister, we should check ourselves and make sure not to speak with bitterness or anger. Shining light on someone should be illuminated in love, or we risk pushing that person further in to darkness.

Today, I will remember judgement is not mine to give. Father help me, that my words don't come out as critical or judgmental. If I witness my brother or sister hurting themselves or others, I will speak from the foundation of love. Only then will my words be heard.

John 8:16, NKJV

"And yet if I do judge, my judgement is true; for I am not alone, but I am with the Father who sent me."

John 8:4-5, NKJV

After hearing Jesus, and convicted by their conscience, they went out one by one, casting no stones.

Unanswered Prayers

If I regard iniquity in my heart, The Lord will not hear.
—Psalms 66:18, NKJV

If we are seeking God's will and asking in our petitions for things that will glorify Him, then our prayers will be answered. However, just as a child makes a request that might harm them and will not be in their best interest, our Father in heaven knows when our prayers should go unanswered. God, who knows all and sees our futures, will protect us against certain requests. Even though He is sovereign and could answer every prayer, He loves us too much to do that.

We need to be thankful for unanswered prayers. When we look back, we will recognize the requests that weren't in His plan for our lives. He does answer anything that we ask, according to His will and purpose for our life. However, if we are asking outside of His will for our lives or when He knows the timing isn't right, our prayers will go unanswered.

We are also told to persevere. If we are praying for something in God's will, it also needs to be in His time. If we pray without answer and believe in our spirit through discernment that our petition is correct, then we should continue in fervent prayer. When prayers are still not answered but we believe they are in God's will, we should seek council from an elder or mature believer to guide us.

Another reason for unanswered prayers is when we are living in disobedience. We must take an honest look at our lives and ask, "Is there inequity or sin in our hearts?" If this is the case, we need to reconcile what is blocking our prayers. Finally, we need to make sure our hearts are pure and humble, and our requests are without vanity or pride.

As we become sanctified in Christ, we will start to recognize the requests we've made that our Heavenly Father knew weren't the best thing for us. Filled with discernment we will know what we should pray for and be grateful for His sovereignty and unanswered prayers.

Today, I give thanks for my unanswered prayers. I trust, Father, that You know what is best and will answer my prayers according to Your will. Please give me the discernment I need to learn Your will and what to pray for.

James 4:3, NKJV

You ask and do not receive, because you ask amiss, that you may spend it on your pleasures.

Psalms 66:18, NKJV

If I regard iniquity in my heart, The Lord will not hear.

1 John 5:14, NKJV

Now this is the confidence that we have in Him, that if we ask anything according to His will, He hears us.

A Castle Made of Sand

Therefore, whoever hears these sayings of Mine, and does them, I will liken him to a wise man who built his house on the rock: and the rain descended, the floods came, and the winds blew and beat on that house; and it did not fall, for it was founded on the rock. But everyone who hears these sayings of Mine, and does not do them, will be like a foolish man who built his house on the sand: and the rain descended, the floods came, and the winds blew and beat on that house; and it fell. And great was its fall.

—Matthew 7:24-27, NKJV

The foundation of God is solely found from His Word. We can attend church every Sunday and pray every day; but if we do not seek His word, our foundation can be likened to a "castle made of sand." When we first accept Jesus as our Lord and Savior and become filled with the Holy Spirit, we feel emboldened and empowered. It is comparable to our first love, when everything seems right with the world. But as the newness wears off, we can be left feeling empty and weak. That's why it is so important to start reading Scripture as a new Christian.

We must fully understand the gospels, the cannons, and the prophetic books of the Bible. Knowledge of God's Word gives us the power we need to ward off Satan's attacks. If we do not build this solid foundation, our lives and faith are subject to crumble.

Knowing a little is worse than knowing nothing at all. Satan loves a new Christian. For no one knows Scripture better than he or will use it more fervently to cause our fall. He plays the ultimate chess game of life, attempting to win every pawn, before finally being defeated. Satan did not hesitate to tempt Jesus himself. Jesus, knowing He was weak in the body of a man, used God's Word against Satan.

It is disconcerting when the enemy attacks (and he will), for a man alone can't stand against Satan. Only He who stands on the Word of God can stand against the enemy. The word is the cornerstone of our foundation in which we build our house. Brick by brick, passage by passage, we can withstand anything when we truly know the living Word. No matter the storms that come or the temptations, we will never fail, but be delivered through the truth and knowledge we receive by studying and knowing scripture. It is our shield and protection against the principalities of darkness.

Today, I will look at my foundation and ask, "Am I completely rooted in God's word?" I thank You, Jesus, for being my rock and foundation. Please let me stand today and every day, knowing through Your Word my castle is not made of sand.

1 Corinthians 3:11, NKJV

For no other foundation can anyone lay than that which is laid, which is Jesus Christ.

Psalms 18:2, NKJV

The Lord is my rock and my fortress and my deliverer; My God, my strength, in whom I will trust.

Am I Green with Envy?

Take heed and beware of covetousness, for one's life does not consist in the abundance of the things he possesses.
—Luke 12:15, NKJV

It is extremely hard not to envy another's life. Just like the "grass is always greener on the other side," it is easy to compare our lives with those who seem to have it all. Measuring our success by what we have in comparison to the abundance of others will produce envy and jealousy. Envy is never of God, but of the enemy, and we must be very careful of slipping into this kind of thinking. This is hard to avoid when success is measured by who has the fanciest home and the shiniest car, takes the best vacations, and sends their children to the most expensive schools.

Even more frustrating is how often we see this "wealth" belonging to non-believers. We live in a world where we are judged by what we have, not by who we are, and the division between "haves" and "have nots" continues to grow.

Falling into this trap and way of thinking diminishes our life and purpose as followers of Jesus Christ. We cannot serve our Father if envy is in our hearts, and when our focus and devotion is not on Him. We must recognize the stronghold of envy, so strong and sinful it is our Tenth Commandment.

We are commanded by God not to have a covetous heart. Jealousy is the devil telling us we deserve what others possess. It is imperative when this happens that we take hold and resist what the enemy is trying to tell us. Any feelings of inadequacy or desires to have more should immediately be turned over to our Heavenly Father. He will tell us the truth, that everything we have is enough, and, in His time, He will bless us beyond our greatest desires.

Today, I count my blessings, for God is infinite, sovereign, and knows the end to the beginning. I will resist being jealous of others and what they have. When I covet what my neighbor has, I forsake God and what He has given me, which is exactly what I should have at this time.

Job 5:2, NKJV

For wrath kills a foolish man, and envy slays a simple one.

Proverbs 23: 17-18, NKJV

Do not let your heart envy sinners but be zealous for the fear of the Lord all the day; For surely there is a hereafter, and your hope will not be cut off.

Proverbs 14:30, NKJV

A sound heart is life to the body, but envy is rottenness to the bones.

Do Not Wrestle with Evil

And Jesus answered and said to him "Get behind Me, Satan! For it is written, 'You shall worship the Lord your God, and Him Only you shall serve.'"
—Luke 4:8; Duet. 6:13, 10:20, NKJV

When Jesus went into the wilderness for forty days in a human body, He knew not to fight with the devil. He was hungry, thirsty, and weary, and He could not rely on His own strength (in the human body) to resist (or wrestle with) Satan. He used the armor of God, *Scripture*, to protect Himself.

We can't rely on our own human strength or understanding. As new believers, we feel "appointed" to fight against evil and take up our shield and sword for battle. On our own, we will lose every time. We learn (the hard way) how crazy this is to believe our strength can match the enemy's.

Just as Adam and Eve could not resist the temptation to eat from the tree of knowledge, we cannot stand alone against the evil one. We must call upon the Lord for His strength. He will send His angels to protect us and fight the battle; our job is to accept weakness, release our enemies and temptations to Him, and surrender completely. God alone will defeat the devil.

When we do surrender, it is amazing how quickly God deals with our enemies, overcomes evil in our lives, and shines His light on the darkness. Peace comes through surrender and knowledge that our power is in the blood of Christ. In His final words, Jesus proclaimed, "It is finished," and it was. His crucifixion and death were the final battle that defeated evil. We no do not have to wrestle with the principalities of darkness.

Today, I ask my Heavenly Father to keep me from trying to wrestle with the evil one. I will find peace in Your strength and victory over evil that was defeated at the cross. My peace comes through surrender, and I let go of any struggles with the knowledge that You will always protect me and keep me safe from harm.

Isaiah 41:10, NKJV

Fear not, for I am with you; be not dismayed, for I am your God. I will strengthen you, yes, I will help you, I will uphold you with My righteous right hand.

Ephesians 6:12, NKJV

For we do not wrestle against flesh and blood, but against principalities, against powers, against the rulers of the darkness of this age, against spiritual hosts of wickedness in the heavenly places. Therefore, take up the whole armor of God, that you may be able to withstand in the evil day, and having done all, to stand.

Philippians 4:13, NKJV

For I can do all things through Christ who strengthens me.

I Will Ask for Wisdom, Anointing and Favor!
—Pat Robertson

A good man obtains favor from the Lord.

—Proverbs 12:2, NKVJ

I love the answer that Pat Robertson gave when asked, "what did he pray for?" He answered, "Wisdom, anointing and favor; all of these according to God's will." The key to receiving His blessings is living a life of obedience, that is pleasing to Him. Then, when we ask for blessings in His name and according to His will, our cups will overflow.

Jesus tells us, when we ask anything in His name, it will be given to us. In the book of James, we are told, if any of you lacks wisdom, let him ask of God, who gives to all liberally and without reproach, and it will be given to him (see scriptures below).

This is a very short and simple message. As followers of Jesus Christ, we are all worthy to ask for wisdom, anointing, and favor. There should be no guilt associated with asking these things from our Heavenly Father, who wants to bless us with all things.

Today, I will not feel guilty asking for blessings in my own life, for I know my heavenly Father wants me to prosper. If living according to His will, I can ask for wisdom, anointing, and favor. Please Father, let me live a life that is pleasing to You. I give thanks for everything He has in store for me and celebrate how awesome it is to be a child of God.

2 Corinthians 9:8, NKJV

And God is able to make all grace abound toward you, that you, always having all sufficiency in all things, may have an abundance for every good work.

Luke 11:9-10, NKJV

"So, I say to you, ask, and it will be given to you; seek, and you will find; knock, and it will be opened to you. For everyone who asks receives, and he who seeks finds, and to him who knocks it will be opened."

James 1:5, NKJV

If any of you lacks wisdom, let him ask of God, who gives to all liberally and without reproach, and it will be given to him.

John 10:10, NKJV

"The thief does not come except to steal, and to kill, and to destroy. I have come that they may have life, and that they may have it more abundantly.

God Loves Me as He Loves Christ!

You have sent Me, and have loved them as You have loved Me.

—John 18:23, NKJV

What an amazing sensation! Feeling the unconditional, unequivocal love of my Heavenly Father. God loves you because it's in His character. He loves us not because of duty, but because it's who He is and what He does. He loves us with perfect, unconditional love. It is the love of God that drives us. The love of God keeps us disciplined and on the right path. His love gives us a desire to keep pushing when struggling with sin.

God is never mad at us. Whenever we think that we have done something to separate ourselves from God's love, He waits for us to come back to Him. Nothing will ever separate us from His love. His love is eternal.

The love of God transforms us.

This message in and of itself, is finite. If there is only one message, one truth you take away from this book, let it be *God loves you!*

Today, Father, I pray for a better understanding of Your infinite love. To be in Your presence, and feel this overwhelming, perfect, unconditional love is all that I need. May I never forget the sacrifice of Your only begotten Son; the ultimate confirmation of Your love for me.

Though our feelings come and go, God's love for us does not.

—*C.S. Lewis*

1 John 3: 1, NKJV

Behold what manner of love the Father has bestowed on us, that we should be called children of God! Therefore, the world does not know us, because it did not know Him.

John 3:16, NKJV

For God so loved the world that He gave His only begotten Son, that whoever believes in Him should not perish but have everlasting life.

2 Thessalonians 3:5, NKJV

Now may the Lord direct your hearts into the love of God and into the patience of Christ.

Romans 8:38, NKJV

For I am persuaded that neither death nor life, nor angels nor principalities nor powers, nor things present nor things to come, nor height nor depth, nor any other created thing, shall be able to separate us from the love of God which is in Christ Jesus our Lord.

1 Corinthians 13: 4-8, NKJV

Love suffers long and is kind; love does not envy; love does not parade itself, is not puffed up; does not behave rudely, does not seek its own, is not provoked, thins no evil; does not rejoice in iniquity, but rejoices in the truth; bears all things, believes all things, hopes all things, endures all things. Love never fails...

"Teach Your Children"

You, who are on the road,
Must have a code that you can live by.
And so become yourself
Because the past is just a good-bye.
Teach your children well,
Their father's hell did slowly go by,
And feed them on your dreams,
The one they pick, the one you'll know by.
Don't you ever ask them why, if they told you, you will
    cry,
So just look at them and sigh
And know they love you.
And you, of tender years,
Can't know the fears that your elders grew by.
And so please help them with your youth,
They seek the truth before they can die.
Teach your parents well,

Their children's hell will slowly go by,
And feed them on your dreams,
The one they pick, the one you'll know by.
Don't you ever ask them why, if they told you, you will
*   cry,*
So just look at them and sigh
And know they love you.
  —Graham Nash, "Teach Your Children"

Graham Nash wrote this song in 1968, when he was with the Hollies. Unimpressed by the lyrics, the Hollies never recorded it, but later with Crosby, Stills, Nash and Young, it was recorded and become one of their biggest hits. It is about the relationship he had with his abusive father, who was in and out of prison during Grahams' childhood. I can't find anything that suggests Graham Nash was (or is) a Christian, but regardless, the words tell a very poignant story of a child who under the worst of circumstances has an everlasting bond with his parent. No matter what abuse or horrors he may have faced, he still loved his father unconditionally. It's about pain and heartache put on a child who has no choice in the family he was born into. It also speaks to generational curses that get passed from father to son and finding forgiveness and truth, as well as setting the father free before he dies. The lyrics are about reconciliation and healing, correcting the mistakes that both father and son made.

Children are no mistake or accident. The day of their birth was long ago determined by God. They are His greatest gift that He entrusts us with for a season. They are given to us as a blank slate, and it is our responsibility not only to provide them nourishment for their physical well-being, but also to nurture their spirit and soul. If we do not do these things simultaneously from birth, our children can't fully embrace life and will be unbalanced adults.

Just as a soldier must be fully trained before going into war, we must prepare our children to face the battlefields of this world. It is never too late to teach them to love their heavenly Father, but it becomes much more difficult the longer we wait. Our focus and prayers for our children should always be that they will live a sanctified life. There is nothing more important in life as a parent than to secure our children's happiness, well-being, and love for Christ.

Father, let me not fail my children but prepare them for this world. I will teach them to love and fear You, and I will instruct them on how to live a sanctified, blessed life. They will learn through my actions how to worship You, tithe, and be a true follower of Jesus Christ. It starts and ends with me. Thank You for entrusting me with Your greatest gift and blessing.

Proverbs 22:6, NKJV

Train up a child in the way he should go, and when he is old, he will not depart from it.

Ephesians 6:4, NKJV

And you fathers, do not provoke your children to wrath, but bring them up in the training and admonition of the Lord.

Psalms 127:3, NLV

See, children are a gift from the Lord. The children born to us are our special reward.

A True Friend

*A man who has friends must himself be friendly, but there
is a friend who sticks closer than a brother.*
—Proverbs 18:24, NKJV

Friendship is truly one of the greatest gifts in life. In
our friends we find trusted companions who know us
and love us for who we are, no matter what. Our friends
are the people who get us through rough times—the
people who come to us with compassion and good counsel. If we have one true friend in our lifetime, we should
be very grateful. They are the ones who never give up on
us, even if we go down the wrong path. They will never gossip or speak behind our backs. A true friend will
wait if they are troubled and approach us privately and
with love. They are the people who, regardless of how
much time may go by, step right back in our lives and
love us unconditionally.

Friendship can also be challenging and messy, as it
takes a lot of work to keep relationships with friends

happy and healthy. I have personally struggled with friendship my entire life. I've had hundreds of acquaintances who befriended me when times were good but very few who stayed by my side when things were bad. It has taken decades to recognize my true friends and what they mean to me. I finally see what a true friendship means.

When we are blessed with a true friend, it is so important that we guard that friendship with our lives. We should nurture and cherish our friendships and let them know just how precious they are and how much we love them. This is why Scripture tells us there is no greater love than to lay down your life for a friend.

Today, I give thanks for the greatest gift, a true friend. I will reach out to tell them what a blessing they are in my life. Father, give me the discernment I need to recognize who my true friends really are. Separate me from the ones who only want me for what I have, that they may take from me. Protect me against those who mean harm. Let me be a true friend and do what it takes to nurture and cherish my precious friendship. Give me the kind of friend that I would lay down my life for!

John 15: 13, NKJV

"Greater love has no one than this, than to lay down one's life for his friends."

Ecclesiastes 4:10, NKJV

For if they fall, one will lift up his companion. But woe to him who is alone when he falls, for he has no one to help him up.

Proverbs 27: 9, NKJV

Oil and perfume delight the heart, and the sweetness of a man's friend gives delight by hearty counsel.

What Should Church Look Like?

For I received from the Lord that which I also delivered to you; that the Lord Jesus on the same night in which He was betrayed took bread; and when He had given thanks, He broke it and said. "take, eat; this is My body which is broken for you; do this in remembrance of Me." In the same manner He also took the cup after supper, saying, "This cup is the new covenant in My blood. This do, as often as you drink it, in remembrance of Me." For as often as you eat this bread and drink this cup, you proclaim the Lord's death till He comes.

—1 Corinthians 11: 23-26 NKJV

Jesus commanded His followers to regularly come together to remember and celebrate His death. A biblical church commemorates this through the Lord's supper, a communal event in which the church publicly proclaims the death and resurrection of Christ. While not expressly forbidden, there isn't a single place in

Scripture where a person celebrates the Lord's supper by themselves.

Church consists of believers coming together, in the same physical space, in the name of Jesus Christ. To gather together in the name of Jesus means gathering together to publicly worship and serve Jesus, and help others know the love of Christ.

The church is a place of spiritual protection. Jesus expects His followers to help one another pursue holiness. If a Christian begins to engage in serious sin, Jesus expects the members of His Christian community to lovingly rebuke them. If the person refuses to repent of sin, the entire church is expected to get involved.

This process presupposes that a Christian will be vitally connected to other Christians. The reality is the process of discipline can't happen apart from a local church. A biblical church not only maintains discipline through corporate worship, but also gives us a place to share our spiritual gifts and build one another up.

It is impossible to build other Christians up if we're not regularly gathering together with other Christians in the context of corporate worship. We are also told to address one another with our psalms, hymns, and spiritual songs. When the church gathers to sing, we are proclaiming truth to one another. He wants us to proclaim his goodness and glory to Him and each other through song and worship.

In a post-modern, democratic society, none of these ideas are very popular, but they are biblical. We live in a time where many "churches" are not teaching biblical principles and are more like social gatherings. The sermons are "motivational messages," specifically designed for the masses, to make us comfortable and feel good. A true biblical message should make us uncomfortable as it addresses our sins and shortcomings.

It is up to each of us to find a biblical church, whether it be two believers or an entire congregation to celebrate Christ. Through the Holy Spirit, we are given the wisdom and discernment to recognize what this should look like. We are also warned not to follow false doctrine, meaning God expects us to know Scripture and the message of the Gospel. A biblical church will be led by qualified elders and the leader or pastor should be beyond reproach.

Today, Heavenly Father, let me recognize what church should look like. Let me ask myself, "Am I worshipping at the right place?" Give me the discernment to see that I am attending a biblical church and, if not, the courage to change my place of worship.

Ephesians 5:18-20, NKJV

And do not be drunk with wine, in which is dissipation; but be filled with the Spirit, speaking to one another in psalms and hymns and spiritual sons, singing and making melody in your heart to the Lord, giving thanks always for all things to God the Father in the name of our Lord Jesus Christ.

1 Corinthians 14:26, NKJV

How is it then brethren: Whenever you come together, each of has a psalm, has a teaching, has a tongue, has a revelation, has an interpretation. Let all things be done for edification.

2 Timothy 4: 3-4, NKJV

For the time will come when they will not endure sound doctrine, but according to their own desires, because they have itching ears, they will heap up for themselves teachers; and they will turn their ears away from the truth and be turned aside to fables.

Signed, Sealed, Delivered

And we know that all things work together for good to those who love God, to those who are the called according to His purpose.

—Romans 8:28, NKJV

God chose us before the creation and foundation of the world. In Him, we are signed into the spirit of promise. We are sealed as a child of God. No one can break this seal that has been purchased by the blood of Christ. We have been delivered to accomplish whatever He has in store for us. He has equipped all of us according to these gifts.

Nothing happens to us without His knowledge, and He is always present. But if we have gone astray, He must work to get us back on track and that won't be without pain or suffering. All He wants for us is peace (to bind together) with Him. *His* love and *His* Peace. He will get us through the suffering we've brought upon ourselves, but in *His* time.

God is always there, including when we have totally screwed things up! When He corrects us, He is undoing the wrongs we've committed, and that can't be in an instant. Our future is so beyond what we can see, and what we go through may hurt and cause pain, but He's working through our problems and making us whole again.

When we read His word, we learn what He can do and will get a whole different opinion on who He is. We will see that He feels what we feel and understands what we are going through. We will understand that He shed the blood of His only Son for us! When we accept Jesus Christ as our Lord and Savior, we are signed, sealed, and delivered as a child of God.

Today, I ask, "Do I schedule prayer every day with my Father in Heaven? Am I abiding by His laws and keeping His commandments? Am I living a life that reflects the life of Christ? Do I humble myself before my Father in Heaven and admit all of my sins? Am I obeying God and leaving all of the consequences to Him? Am I walking in His will? Do I desire to please Him and trust Him in every circumstance? Do I wait upon the Lord?" Father, please, let me be signed, sealed and delivered through the blood of Jesus.

John 14:21, NKJV

"He who has My commandments and keeps them, it is he who loves Me. And he who loves Me will be loved by My Father, and I will love him and manifest Myself to him.

Philippians 4:19, NKJV

And my God shall supply all your need according to His riches in glory by Christ Jesus.

Ephesians 1:13, NKJV

In Him you also trusted, after you heard the word of truth, the gospel of your salvation; in whom also, having believed, you were sealed with the Holy Spirit of promise, who is the guarantee of our inheritance until the redemption of the purchased possession, to the praise of His glory.

1 John 1:7-9, NKJV

But if we walk in the light as He is in the light, we have fellowship with one another, and the blood of Jesus Christ His Son cleanses us from all sin. If we say that we have no sin, we deceive ourselves, and the truth is not in us. If we confess our sins, He is faithful and just to forgive us our sins and to cleanse us from all unrighteousness.

What Does the
Future Hold?

*But of that day and hour no one knows, not even the angels
in heaven, nor the Son, but only the Father. Take heed, watch
and pray; for you do not know when the time is.*
—Mark 13: 32-33, NKJV

We all have a final destination: heaven or hell. As far
as the second coming, it can be at any minute. The time
is already set; the prophesies fulfilled. Jesus could come
back at the "twinkling of an eye," and "like a thief in the
night."

The Second Coming of Jesus is a subject that most
churches, choose to ignore, leaving their congregations
with very little information or understanding. On the
other side of the spectrum are religions that make the
second coming their entire focus and doctrine. Regardless, each of us need to have a comprehensive understanding about this coming event.

First and foremost, there's nothing to worry about or fear if you are a believer and follower of Jesus Christ. Second, there's no amount of preparing, stock piling food and money, or securing properties that can save us from what's to come. We can only prepare our souls through constant prayer and worship.

When Jesus comes, there will be suffering, world-wide confusion, economic uncertainty, wars, and extreme cultural division. But only when every person on this planet has had an opportunity to know, reject or accept Christ as their Savior, will He come for us.

Jesus' own disciples believed He would come back in their lifetime. The truth of the second coming is no one knows when this event will happen, although there will be signs. Jesus tells His disciples that even He does not know when the time or hour will be. He only says that when it is near, things will be so bad here on earth, He will beg the Father to send Him and to end the suffering.

Jesus tells His disciples to "keep watch." Then tells the parable of the ten virgins in the book of Matthew, chapter 25. The story concludes with the door to the wedding feast being closed to the half of the maidens who were not prepared. This door represents the gates of Heaven and is a warning to those who do not repent before the second coming. If you have accepted Jesus as your Lord and Savior and repented of all your sins, you have the promise of Heaven. Believers have no reason to worry about what the future holds.

Today, let me look at my heart and ask, "Am I ready for the second coming?" "Have I accepted Christ as my Savior, and repented of all of my sins?" If so, I know what my future holds. Eternal life without suffering, where I will be with my Heavenly Father. If my soul is prepared, then I am ready for the second coming. Thank You, Father, for Your amazing promise of Heaven!

Matthew 25: 1-13, NKJV

Then the kingdom of heaven shall be likened to ten virgins who took their lamps and went out to meet the bridegroom. Now five of them were wise, and five were foolish. Those who were foolish took their lamps and took no oil with them, but the wise took oil in their vessels with their lamps. But while the bridegroom was delayed, they all slumbered and slept. And at midnight a cry was heard: Behold, the bridegroom is coming; go out to meet him? Then all those virgins arose and trimmed their lamps. And the foolish said to the wise, "Give us some of your oil, for our lamps are going out." But the wise answered, saying "No, lest there should not be enough for us and you, but go rather to those who sell, and buy for yourselves." And while they went to buy, the bridegroom came, and those who were ready went in with him to the wedding; and the door was shut. Afterward the other virgins came also, saying, "Lord, Lord, open to us!" But he answered and said, "Assuredly, I say

to you, I do not know you." Watch therefore, for you know nei-
ther the day nor the hour in which the Son of Man is coming.

Who is Christ?

He said to them, "But who do you say that I am?" Peter
answered and said, "The Christ of God."
— Luke 9:20, NKJV

When we become believers and followers of Jesus
Christ, we will immediately be challenged on our position by the secular world and must be able to answer,
"Who is Christ?" If we cannot answer this question with
total conviction and authority, we will miss many opportunities to bring others to salvation. When we first
become a Christian, reading the Bible may seem daunt-
ing. The questions of "where do I start?" and "how do I
interpret what it says?" are just a few of many questions
we ask ourselves.

What I have learned is we all have to start some-
where, and that doesn't mean starting at the first page
and not stopping until we reach page 1131. When I first
became a Christian, I would randomly open the Bible
and start reading. It's amazing how often that I turned

to a page with the exact message God wanted me to hear!

A new Christian should start with the gospels. The book of John is probably the most personal account of the life of Jesus Christ. The book of Luke gives an historical account, laying out the genealogy of Jesus. While studying the gospels, we should also be reading the book of Psalms. There's no required pace, and the Holy Spirit will lead you. Even if you start with five minutes a day and work your way up, it will move you towards a solid foundation and unwavering faith.

Here is the answer: Christ is the King of Kings, Lord of Lords, King of the Jews, Son of Man, Immanuel, Shepherd of the flock, the Lord of Righteousness, the Lamb, Prince of Peace, the Alpha and the Omega, our Savior, the Leader of all nations, the Leader of the universe, the Judge and Jury, the Holy Trinity, and Father, Son and Holy Ghost. He is the Son of God and without sin. He came the first time to offer salvation and will come the second time to give judgement to the entire world.

I am including many scriptures that answer this question and encourage the reader to reference each scripture and read the entire chapter. This will lead to a much clearer understanding and context of the message and prepare you to answer with total confidence; "Who Is Christ?"

Today, I will open the Bible and read the Word. Father, help guide me through and understand your message. Give me the discipline to read daily. Equip me to handle the most important question I will ever answer: "Who is Christ?"

Mark 15:2, NKJV

Then Pilate asked Him, "Are You the King of the Jews?" He answered and said to him, "It is as you say."

Luke 22:70, NKJV

Then they all said, "Are You the Son of God?" So, He said to them, "You rightly say that I am."

Isaiah 53:5, NKJV

But he was wounded for our transgressions, He was bruised for our iniquities; The chastisement for our peace was upon Him, And by His stripes we are healed.

Revelations 17:14, NKJV

These will make war with the Lamb, and the Lamb will overcome them, for He is Lord of lords and King of kings; and those who are with Him are called, chosen, and faithful.

Philippians 2: 8-11, NKJV

And being found in appearance as a man, He humbled Himself and became obedient to the point of death, even the death of the cross. Therefore, God also has highly exalted Him and given Him the name, which is above every name, that at the name of Jesus every knee should bow, of those in heaven, and of those on earth, and of those under the earth, and that every tongue should confess that Jesus Christ is Lord, to the glory of God the Father.

Isaiah 9:6, NKJV

For unto us a Child is born, unto us a Son is given: And the government will be upon His shoulder, and His name will be called Wonderful, Counselor, Mighty God, Everlasting Father, Price of Peace.

Revelations 22:13, NKJV

I am the Alpha and the Omega, the Beginning and the End, the First and the Last.

Matthew 27:37, NKJV

And they put up over His head the accusation written against Him: THIS IS JESUS THE KING OF THE JEWS.

Matthew 27:54, NKJV

So, when the centurion and those with him, who were guarding Jesus, saw the earthquake and the things that had happened, they feared greatly, saying, "Truly this was the Son of God!"

Matthew 2: 1-2, NKJV

Now after Jesus was born in Bethlehem of Judea in the days of Herod the king, behold, wise men from the East came to Jerusalem, saying, "Where is He who has been born King of the Jews? For we have seen His star in the East and have come to worship Him."

Isaiah 7:14, NKJV

Therefore, the Lord Himself will give you a sign: Behold, the virgin shall conceive and bear a Son, and shall call His name Immanuel.

Jeremiah 23:5-6, NKJV

Behold, the days are coming," says the Lord, "That I will raise to David a Branch of righteousness; A King shall reign and prosper and execute judgment and righteousness in the earth. In His days Judah will be saved, and Israel will dwell safely; Now this is His name by which He will be called: THE LORD OUR RIGHTEOUSNESS.

One Body of Christ, One Blood

If anyone says, "I love God," and hates his brother, he is
a liar; for he who does not love his brother whom he has seen
cannot love God whom he has not seen.
—1 John 4:20, NKJV

We cannot be followers of Jesus Christ and hold prejudice in our hearts. The two do not coexist, in fact, they are diabolically opposed. Anyone who claims to be a superior race and has hatred towards others who look different, aren't following the doctrine of Christ, but the doctrine of the Antichrist. If we believe that God created the universe and made Adam and Eve, then we must accept that the human race has one father and one mother. Beyond the pigmentation of our skin is one blood and one body unified in Christ.

We know from Scripture there has always been cultural differences, but there is nothing in the Bible that substantiates these were caused by the color of one's skin. Racism has been developed over centuries by Man, and it is completely superficial.

No one is born with prejudice or bigotry. It is something that is learned, passed on from generation to generation. Fear of the unknown or unfamiliarity fuels bias and hatred. Systemic racism has been going on since our country was founded, even though our forefathers wrote, "All men are created equal" in the Declaration. They knew that equality comes from God, not man. Until we love God and love one another with God's love, we can't have acceptance of one another. Until we embrace the work of the cross, mankind will continue to be prejudice.

When Jesus says, "love our neighbors as ourselves," He knows that as human beings, we show preferential treatment to ourselves and others that look and think the same. He also knows there is no one we think about more or care about better than ourselves. That is why He used this as the standard for how to love other people.

God doesn't give us a long list of rules and regulations or a manual explaining exactly how we should act in every situation. But, His commandment, often referred to as "the golden rule," encompasses everything we need to know. Simply put, love as you want to be loved and love others as you love yourself.

So, what can each of us do to end prejudice? We can embrace the cross of Christ on which there is no distinction of color or race. It's time we stand up and stop accepting and allowing bad things to happen to our sisters and brothers of color. We must pray for change of our own hearts and practice the golden rule.

Dr. Charles Montgomery, a servant of the Lord, recently led a morning devotion and left his audience with a simple charge: Start where you are, use what you have, do what you can.

The great Mother Teresa once said in response to the overwhelming needs she saw everywhere around her, "If you can't feed a hundred people, then feed just one." We can't fix everything or everyone, but we can *do something*. As we change our own hearts and be an example as a servant of Christ, we will affect change in others. We can make a difference and start healing our nation as we come together as one.

Today, I ask the Father to remove all prejudice, bias, and hatred from my heart. I pray for the strength to affect change in others who inflict pain and suffering on brothers and sisters of a different color. I will live by the golden rule and love others, even those who are different from me, as I love myself.

Genesis 3:20, NKJV

And Adam called his wife's name Eve, because she was the mother of all living.

Acts 17:26, NKJV

And He has made from one blood every nation of men to dwell on all the face of the earth.

Batteries Sold Seperately

You comprehend my path and my lying down and are acquainted with all my ways.

—Psalms 139:3, NKJV

Most of us can relate to buying a gift, bringing it home, and realizing the batteries were not included, the manual is missing, or the instructions are too difficult to follow. If time has run out, perhaps it's late Christmas Eve, we go ahead and give our gift with the promise of purchasing the batteries or putting it together later.

When this happens with children, they will be excited about the gift at first, but once they realize they can't play with it, put it away on a shelf, maybe a closet, and eventually forget all about it. It's very possible that once we get around to buying the batteries or putting the toy together, that the child has completely lost interest.

When we first receive the gift of salvation, we have overwhelming feelings of elation and hope. The body of the church surrounds us as we are led to accept Jesus as our Lord and Savior, abandon our old selves, and become new creations in Christ.

The body of Christ (the church) focuses on salvation. They teach us God's infinite laws and moral laws. We learn of His infinite laws of following the Ten Commandments: do not commit murder, adultery, theft, false witness or covet. The moral laws of how we should behave—do not live a life of sexual immorality, gossip, be a drunkard, do not worship money, be a good steward, tithe, and serve the community. We are taught to love others, including our enemies.

What the church rarely teaches us is what to do after receiving Christ. We lack instructions on how to put our newfound faith into action and live a sanctified life. For this reason, many believers fall short of the glory of God and often taper or fall away from Him. It's just as a child will soon discard a toy he can't play with. Once we're past the elation that our new faith brings us but don't know how to use it, we are left with frustration and despair. This is the most prevalent reason people will turn away from the church and fall back into their old patterns.

Finding our purpose, God's will for our lives, and how we attain that, is such an integral part to our salvation. We receive the gift, but the batteries and manual on how to follow Jesus on a daily basis, are not included. Left alone, it is almost impossible to move forward.

There is no "secret formula" or complicated plan to find God's will and a purpose driven life. Once we accept Christ as our Lord and Savior, the very next step is to start praying, asking our Heavenly Father to reveal His purpose for our lives. Just as He put people and situations before us to seek Him and become followers of Jesus, He will start putting people and situations before us to see His will for us. Once we ask, He will open new doors and show us opportunities we've never seen before. God will show us the benefits of following His laws and living a sanctified life.

All we have to do is follow His lead, and He will direct us down the right path. Then we will experience all that He has planned for us, and find a burden free life, full of possibilities. Once we are on His path and fulfilling our destiny according to His will, we develop a new "moral compass," that guides us away from sin and towards righteousness.

Today, I ask my Heavenly Father to reveal His will for me, to fulfill my purpose according to His riches and glory. I will not dwell on time lost but concentrate on my bright future living a purpose driven life. As I pray for His will, I will open my eyes, ears, and heart and look forward to what He puts before me, the opportunities He will give me. I will live my life according to His will and purpose and celebrate the joy, contentment, and satisfaction of living a truly sanctified life.

Ephesians 2:10, NKJV

For we are His workmanship, created in Christ Jesus for good works, which God prepared beforehand that we should walk in them.

Psalms 32:8, NKJV

I will instruct you and teach you in the way you should go; I will guide you with My eye.

Proverbs 19:20, NKJV

Listen to counsel and receive instruction, that you may be wise in your latter years.

Our Final Destination

*For behold, I create new heavens and a new earth; and the
former shall not be remembered or come to mind.*
—Isaiah 65:17, NKJV

None of us can even begin to imagine Heaven and
the glory and joy we will feel. The band Mercy Me does
a great job showing just how amazing the day will be,
when we finally get to meet our Lord and Savior face
to face.

"I Can Only Imagine" – Bart Marshall Miller

> *I can only imagine what it will be like*
> *When I walk, by your side*
> *I can only imagine what my eyes will see*
> *When you face is before me*
> *I can only imagine*

I can only imagine
Surrounded by You glory
What will my heart feel
Will I dance for you Jesus
Or in awe of You be still
Will I stand in your presence
Or to my knees will I fall
Will I sing hallelujah
Will I be able to speak at all
I can only imagine
I can only imagine
I can only imagine when that day comes
When I find myself standing in the Son
I can only imagine when all I would do is forever
Forever worship You
I can only imagine
I can only imagine
Surrounded by Your glory
What will my heart feel
Will I dance for You, Jesus
Or in awe of you be still
Will I stand in your presence
Or to my knees will I fall

Today, Father, I look forward to my forever, worshiping You in all of Your glory. I can only imagine that day and wait anxiously for when we meet face to face!

Revelations 21:4, NKJV

"And God will wipe away every tear from their eyes; there shall be no more death, nor sorrow, nor crying. There shall be no more pain, for the former things have passed away."

Epilogue

If my readers walk away with one thing from this book, I hope they understand life is about choices. God blesses us with free will, and it is up to each of us how we *choose* to live our life.

We can be positive or negative, happy or sad, live in darkness or choose to live in light. Nothing is too big or impossible for our loving Father, and through Him we can overcome disease, depression, addiction or anything that is blocking us from the joyous, blessed life He has in store for all of His Children.

I think the lyrics from the song, "Ac-Cent-Tchu-Ate the Positive," by the Andrew Sisters reflect my hope for the reader and gives a light-hearted message on how followers of Jesus Christ should live.

On a more serious side, Jesus warns us in the book of Revelations not to be lukewarm in our beliefs. He is telling us, there is no "in-between."

God tells us He puts before us life or death, blessing or cursing, but we **must choose**, pick a side and stand together. *We **can** turn the page, turning from darkness to light through Christ Jesus!*

"Ac-Cent-Tchu-Ate the Positive" —The Andrew Sisters

You've got to accentuate the positive
Eliminate the negative
Latch on to the affirmative
Don't mess with Mister In-Between
You've got to spread joy up to the maximum
Bring gloom down to the minimum
Have faith or pandemonium
Liable to walk upon the scene
To illustrate his last remark
Jonah in the whale, Noah in the ark
What did they do
Just when everything looked so dark
Man, they said we better, accentuate the positive
Eliminate the negative
Latch on to the affirmative
Don't mess with Mister In-Between
No, do not mess with Mister In-Between
Do you hear me?
Oh, listen to me children and you will hear
About the elininatin' of the negative
And the accent on the positive
And gather 'round me children if you're willin'

And sit tight while I start reviewin'
the positive....

Revelations 3:15-16, ESV

"I know your works: you are neither cold nor hot. Would that you were either cold or hot! So, because you are lukewarm, and neither hot nor cold, I will spit you out of my mouth.

About the Author

Anne Maxwell's writings are a reflection of her personal struggles as she tries to reconcile how to live a sanctified life in an unsanctified world. She spent thirty-five years in the corporate world, living to work, and focusing on success and financial gains. Finding no satisfaction or happiness, she started her spiritual journey which led to retiring from a high-pressured sales job to running her own business. She now works to live and spends time enjoying her relationship with Jesus Christ, family, and friends.

Anne was raised in The First Presbyterian Church and has conservative theological views reflected in this manuscript. However, all of the writings are biblically based. Her hope for the reader, is they will move through each message slowly and have access to the Bible to reference and study the scriptures in their full context.

The messages in this book are based on the answers she found through years of determined Bible study, memorizing scripture, listening to Christian programs, and journaling. Turn the Page was a healing process for her, and she prays it will be for others. She prays that her readers will find answers to their own questions or struggles in life and turn from darkness to light through Christ Jesus.

Endnotes

1 "Light," Merriam-Webster, 8 Nov. 2020, https://www.merriam-webster.com/dictionary/light.

2 "Dark," Merriam-Webster, 4 Nov. 2020, https://www.merriam-webster.com/dictionary/dark.

3 James Strong, *The Exhaustive Concordance of the Bible*, 1890 (USA, republished to this day)

4 John Newton, *Thoughts Upon the African Slave Trade*, 1788 (London, United Kingdom)

5 "Sheol," Wikipedia, 31 October 2020, https://en.wikipedia.org/wiki/Sheol.

6 "Reciprocity," Merriam-Webster, 30 Oct. 2020, https://www.merriam-webster.com/dictionary/reciprocity.

7 "Tithe," Merriam-Webster, 10 Sept. 2020, https://www.merriam-webster.com/dictionary/tithe.

8 "Strife," Merriam-Webster, 6 Nov. 2020, https://www.merriam-webster.com/dictionary/strife.